Better Homes and Gardens®

VEGETABLES

BETTER HOMES AND GARDENS® BOOKS

Editor Gerald M. Knox
Art Director Ernest Shelton
Managing Editor David A. Kirchner
Copy and Production Editors James D. Blume, Marsha Jahns, Rosanne Weber Mattson, Mary Helen Schiltz

Food and Nutrition Editor Nancy Byal
Department Head, Cook Books Sharyl Heiken
Associate Department Heads Sandra Granseth, Rosemary C. Hutchinson, Elizabeth Woolever
Senior Food Editors Julia Malloy, Marcia Stanley, Joyce Trollope
Associate Food Editors Linda Henry, Mary Major, Diana McMillen, Mary Jo Plutt, Maureen Powers, Martha Schiel, Linda Foley Woodrum
Recipe Development Editor Marion Viall
Test Kitchen Director Sharon Stilwell
Test Kitchen Photo Studio Director Janet Pittman
Test Kitchen Home Economists Lynn Blanchard, Jean Brekke, Kay Cargill, Marilyn Cornelius, Jennifer Darling, Maryellyn Krantz, Lynelle Munn, Dianna Nolin, Marge Steenson

Associate Art Directors Linda Ford Vermie, Neoma Alt West, Randall Yontz
Assistant Art Directors Lynda Haupert, Harijs Priekulis, Tom Wegner
Senior Graphic Designers Jack Murphy, Stan Sams, Darla Whipple-Frain
Graphic Designers Mike Burns, Blake Welch, Brian Wignall

Vice President, Editorial Director Doris Eby
Executive Director, Editorial Services Duane L. Gregg

President, Book Group Fred Stines
Director of Publishing Robert B. Nelson
Vice President, Retail Marketing Jamie Martin
Vice President, Direct Marketing Arthur Heydendael

Vegetables
Editor Maureen Powers
Copy and Production Editor Mary Helen Schiltz
Graphic Designer Harijs Priekulis
Electronic Text Processor Donna Russell
Photographers Michael Jensen and Sean Fitzgerald
Food Stylists Suzanne Finley, Carol Grones, Dianna Nolin, Janet Pittman
Contributing Writer Sandra Mosley

On the cover
Caulifower-Asparagus Stir-Fry (see recipe, page 86)

Our seal assures you that every recipe in *Vegetables* has been tested in the Better Homes and Gardens® Test Kitchen. This means that each recipe is practical and reliable, and meets our high standards of taste appeal.

Vegetables, glorious vegetables! Today's interest in health, nutrition, dieting, and eating light is fast making vegetables a favorite dish at any meal—and sometimes they're the *only* dish!

Here you'll rediscover old favorites and get acquainted with an assortment of new and unusual garden goodies. Look for quick-to-fix recipes or upscale, elegant dishes. When you don't need a recipe, easy-to-read charts with simple-to-follow directions let you perfectly cook fresh vegetables at a glance.

From soup to dessert, bread to salad, side dish to main dish, vegetables make a strong stand in the hearts of food lovers. One sample from *Vegetables* and we're sure you'll want to give your own "taste-amony" to these vegetable recipes that make the most of nature's abundant harvest.

Contents

Introduction
3

**Vegetables That
Go Crunch**
6

Garden-fresh flavor and
crunch shine in an array of
salads and appetizers.

**The Best
Of Boiling**
12

Easy boiling plus a quick
twist of flavor equals
sensational vegetable dishes.

**Taters and
Toppers**
18

A dozen international
ideas—Mexican, Creole,
Indian, and all-American—
for top-rated baked
potatoes.

**Stuffed
Specialties**
46

Nifty ideas for cooking and
serving vegetables in their
own shells.

**Microwave
Magic**
52

Not only fast, but beautiful
and delicious appetizers,
relishes, salads, and
vegetable side-dishes.

**Simply Smashing
Vegetables**
60

Everything from fancy piped
sweet potatoes to classic
mashed potatoes with lots
of smashing serving ideas in
between.

**Saucy
Vegetables**
66

Smooth, cheesy sauces
become the crowning glory
for your favorite vegetables.

**Pan-Fried
Vegetables**
98

Unique ideas for quick pan-
fried snacks.

**Delectable Deep-
Fried Vegetables**
102

Mouth-watering delights—
homemade potato chips,
french fries, onion rings,
and much, much more.

**Whole-in-
One Pizza**
108

An international winner—
German flavors translated
into an Italian pizza.

**So-Light
Soufflés**
112

Delicate vegetable flavors
embellish airy soufflés.

Scrumptious Soups
24

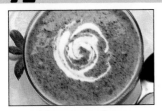

Be it appetizer, main dish, or side dish—we have soups to suit your taste.

Under the Heat
30

The broiler gets into the act and transforms fresh vegetables into unusual fare.

Vegetables from The Bakery
34

You can have your cake and eat your vegetables, too, just by adding shredded vegetables to the batter.

Steaming Along
38

The simple art of steaming produces vegetables rich in color and flavor.

Classy Cream Soups
72

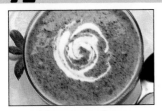

Icy cold or piping hot, creamy soups fill the bill for appetizers or as an accompaniment to sandwiches at lunch.

Hearty Dry Bean Dishes
78

What's for dinner? How about soup, stew, chili, or baked beans?

Say It with A Stir-Fry
84

Main dishes and side dishes are ready in a flash when you stir-fry.

Great for Grilling
92

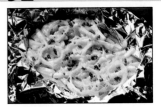

Vegetables cook on the grill right beside the meat.

Cooking Fresh Vegetables
116

Unusual Vegetables
120

Nutrition Analysis Chart
122

Index
125

Special Helps
Easy-to-read information for cooking vegetables including boiling, steaming, broiling, stir-frying, and microwaving.

Special Helps
Now you'll know what they look like, how to store them, and how to prepare unfamiliar vegetables.

Vegetables That Go Crunch

First slice 'em and dice 'em. Then, munch 'em and crunch 'em.

Uncooked vegetables will fit right in with your life-style. Light, fresh, and quick-to-fix, these salads and appetizers cater to busy people looking for healthy, delicious vegetables.

Appetizing Antipasto

Appetizing Antipasto

Whet appetites before dinner or at a party with a beautifully arranged hors d'oeuvre platter of fresh vegetables, meats, and cheeses.

½ pound broccoli *or* cauliflower
2 small yellow crookneck squash
    or zucchini
2 medium carrots
2 small tomatoes
¾ cup pitted ripe olives
⅓ cup olive oil *or* salad oil
¼ cup white wine vinegar
1 tablespoon snipped parsley
1 tablespoon lemon juice
2 teaspoons Dijon-style mustard
½ teaspoon dried basil *or* marjoram,
    crushed
⅛ teaspoon pepper
   Leaf lettuce
4 ounces thinly sliced salami
4 ounces provolone *or* mozzarella cheese,
    cut into sticks
   Melba toast rounds *or* French bread
   (optional)

Wash all vegetables thoroughly. Cut broccoli or cauliflower into flowerets (see photo 1). Bias-slice or thinly slice crookneck squash or zucchini (see photo 2). Cut carrots into julienne strips (see photo 3). Cut tomatoes into thin wedges (see photo 4). In a large bowl combine prepared vegetables and olives.

For marinade, in a screw-top jar combine olive oil or salad oil, vinegar, parsley, lemon juice, mustard, basil or marjoram, and pepper. Cover and shake well (see photo 5). Pour marinade over vegetable mixture; toss to coat. Cover and chill 2 to 24 hours, stirring occasionally to distribute marinade.

Line a serving platter with leaf lettuce. Using a slotted spoon, transfer vegetables and olives to the platter. Fold salami slices in half; arrange salami and cheese sticks on the platter. Serve with Melba toast or French bread, if desired. Makes 6 to 8 servings.

1 Trim the leaves from the broccoli and wash it under cold running water. Cut off just the flowerets with a sharp knife, as shown. Reserve the stalks to use later in soups or casseroles.

2 To bias-slice squash, hold the vegetable firmly against the cutting board. Place a thin, sharp knife atop the vegetable at a 45-degree angle about ¼ inch from the edge. Then cut down and out.

3 To make julienne strips, cut the carrots in half crosswise, then in half lengthwise. Continue cutting the carrots lengthwise to create long, thin strips, as shown.

4 For neat, thin tomato wedges, cut the tomato in half with a serrated knife and remove the core. Then slice the tomato into wedges using a light back-and-forth motion.

5 An easy way to thoroughly mix ingredients is to place them in a jar with a screw-top lid. Tighten the lid on the jar and shake vigorously to combine the ingredients.

Crunchy Jicama Salad

This mock potato salad is easy to make because the jicama (HEE kuh muh) doesn't need to be cooked.

2 cups cubed jicama (see tip, below)
½ cup bias-sliced celery (see photo 2, page 8)
¼ cup chopped onion
2 tablespoons chopped sweet pickle
⅓ cup mayonnaise *or* salad dressing
1 teaspoon sugar
1 teaspoon celery seed
1 teaspoon prepared mustard
1 hard-cooked egg, coarsely chopped
Lettuce leaves
1 hard-cooked egg, sliced (optional)

In a medium bowl combine jicama, celery, onion, and sweet pickle.

For dressing, in a small bowl combine mayonnaise or salad dressing, sugar, celery seed, mustard, and ¼ teaspoon *salt*. Add dressing to jicama mixture; toss to coat. Gently fold in chopped egg. Cover and chill. Spoon salad into lettuce-lined serving bowl. Garnish with hard-cooked egg slices, if desired. Makes 4 servings.

Creamy Curry-Vegetable Salad

Use either daikon (DIKE un) or parsnips in this simple, yet sophicated salad. See pages 120–121 for more helpful hints on using unusual vegetables.

1 small zucchini, cut into julienne strips (see photo 3, page 9)
½ cup julienne strips daikon *or* parsnip (see photo 3, page 9)
½ cup bias-sliced celery (see photo 2, page 8)
½ cup cashews *or* peanuts
⅓ cup plain yogurt
2 tablespoons orange juice
½ teaspoon curry powder

In a medium bowl combine zucchini, daikon or parsnip, celery, and cashews or peanuts.

For dressing, in a small bowl combine plain yogurt, orange juice, and curry powder. Pour dressing over zucchini mixture; toss to coat. Makes 4 servings.

The Cutting Edge

Cubing: Use a chef's knife to cut strips about ½ inch wide. Then cut crosswise to make cubes ½ inch on all sides.

Dicing: Cut the same as for cubing, but make the pieces smaller. Ingredients that are diced are cut into ⅛- to ¼-inch pieces.

Chopping: Cut foods into irregularly shaped pieces about the size of peas using a knife, chopper, blender, or food processor.

Mincing: Use a utility knife or paring knife to cut the food (usually garlic cloves) into very tiny, irregularly shaped pieces.

Cucumber-Spinach Dip with Crudités

Crudités (kroo dee tay) is just a fancy way of saying a selection of raw sliced vegetables.

½ **cup plain yogurt**
½ **cup dairy sour cream**
¼ **teaspoon salt**
¼ **teaspoon dried dillweed**
   Dash bottled hot pepper sauce
½ **cup finely chopped, seeded cucumber**
½ **cup finely chopped spinach *or* lettuce**
   Assorted vegetable dippers*

In a small bowl combine yogurt, sour cream, salt, dillweed, and hot pepper sauce. Stir in cucumber and spinach or lettuce. Cover and chill 2 to 24 hours.

Prepare assorted vegetable dippers or crudités. Seal vegetables in a clear plastic bag or airtight container and chill till serving time.

Place dip in the center of a serving plate. Arrange assorted vegetable dippers around dip. Makes 1½ cups dip (24 servings).

*Choose from broccoli or cauliflower flowerets (see photo 1, page 8), zucchini or yellow crookneck squash slices (see photo 2, page 8), julienne carrots (see photo 3, page 9), cherry tomatoes or tomato wedges (see photo 4, page 9), green onions, fresh mushrooms, and green pepper squares or strips.

Tomato-Mushroom Salad

Tarragon lends a subtle herb flavor.

3 **medium tomatoes *or* 24 cherry tomatoes**
1 **cup sliced fresh mushrooms**
2 **green onions, thinly sliced (about ¼ cup)**
3 **tablespoons olive oil *or* salad oil**
3 **tablespoons vinegar**
1 **tablespoon water**
1 **teaspoon sugar**
¼ **teaspoon dried tarragon, crushed**
   Dash bottled hot pepper sauce
4 **cups torn lettuce, romaine, *or* spinach**

Cut tomatoes into thin wedges (see photo 4, page 9). (*Or,* cut cherry tomatoes in half.) In a medium bowl combine tomatoes, mushrooms, and green onions.

For marinade, in a screw-top jar combine olive oil or salad oil, vinegar, water, sugar, tarragon, and hot pepper sauce. Cover and shake well (see photo 5, page 9). Pour marinade over vegetable mixture; toss gently to coat. Cover and chill 2 to 24 hours, stirring occasionally to distribute marinade.

Place lettuce, romaine, or spinach in a salad bowl. Add marinated vegetable mixture. Toss to coat. Makes 6 servings.

The Best Of Boiling

Simple doesn't mean boring—it means sensational!

Each delectable side dish starts with boiling water and fresh vegetables. After cooking to perfect crisp-tenderness, we jazz up these vegetables with a flash of exciting flavor.

And to think, it's all as easy as boiling water.

Sesame Broccoli

Sesame Broccoli

"Open sesame!" Ali Baba used that phrase to open a secret cave containing valuable treasures. We use sesame seed to open your taste buds to this gem of a recipe.

1 **pound broccoli, cut into spears, *or* one 10-ounce package frozen broccoli spears**
2 **tablespoons butter *or* margarine**
1 **tablespoon sesame seed**
2 **tablespoons diced pimiento**
1 **tablespoon lemon juice**
   Dash pepper
   Lemon slices (optional)

In a medium saucepan bring 1 cup lightly salted water to boiling. Add broccoli (see photo 1). Return to boiling; reduce heat. Cook, covered, for 11 to 12 minutes or till broccoli is crisp-tender (see photo 2). (*Or,* cook frozen broccoli according to package directions.) Drain broccoli (see photo 3). Return broccoli to saucepan.

Meanwhile, in a small skillet melt butter or margarine. Add sesame seed; cook and stir till seeds are light brown (see photo 4). Remove from heat. Add pimiento, lemon juice, and pepper. Pour sesame mixture over broccoli; stir to coat. Transfer to a serving bowl. Garnish with twisted lemon slices, if desired. Makes 4 servings.

1 Lower the broccoli into the saucepan with tongs or a large spoon to avoid splashing boiling water or burning your hands with the steam.

2 Pierce the stalk or toughest part of the vegetable to test for doneness. When a fork will just go into the food easily, the vegetable is *crisp-tender* (that is, tender but still crisp).

3 Place a colander in the sink, then pour the broccoli into the colander. Give the colander a few firm shakes to drain the water from the broccoli.

4 Stir the sesame seeds constantly with a wooden spoon while you are browning them in the hot butter or margarine. When the seeds are light brown, remove the pan from the heat immediately.

Crumb-Capped Green Beans

½ pound green beans *or* one 10-ounce package frozen cut green beans
⅓ cup herb-seasoned stuffing croutons
1 tablespoon butter *or* margarine, melted

Wash fresh green beans; remove ends and strings. Cut beans into 1-inch pieces. In a medium saucepan bring about ½ cup lightly salted water to boiling. Add green beans (see photo 1, page 14). Return to boiling; reduce heat. Cook, covered, for 20 to 25 minutes or till crisp-tender (see photo 2, page 15). (*Or,* cook frozen beans according to package directions.) Drain beans (see photo 3, page 15).

Meanwhile, crush croutons; stir together crouton crumbs and melted butter or margarine. Transfer beans to a serving bowl. Sprinkle crumb mixture atop beans. Makes 4 servings.

Glazed Onions

It's easier to peel pearl onions after they are cooked.

3 cups pearl onions *or* one 16-ounce package frozen small whole onions
2 tablespoons butter *or* margarine
2 tablespoons brown sugar
¼ cup chopped green *or* sweet red pepper

In a medium saucepan bring about ½ cup lightly salted water to boiling; add *unpeeled* onions (see photo 1, page 14). Return to boiling; reduce heat. Cook, covered, about 10 minutes or till just tender (see photo 2, page 15). (*Or,* cook frozen onions according to package directions.) Drain onions (see photo 3, page 15). Cool pearl onions slightly; trim ends and remove skin.

In the same saucepan stir together butter or margarine, brown sugar, and 1 tablespoon *water.* Cook and stir till combined. Add onions and green or red pepper to saucepan. Simmer, uncovered, 10 to 12 minutes or till onions are glazed, stirring occasionally. Makes 4 servings.

Shrimp-Stuffed Artichokes

The art of eating an artichoke is all in your fingers. Pull off a leaf and dunk it into the creamy shrimp dip. Pull the leaf through your teeth, eating only the tender flesh, then discard the remainder of the leaf. Now you're ready for another one!

2 medium artichokes (about 8 ounces each)
Lemon juice
4 ounces frozen cooked shrimp
½ cup dairy sour cream
½ cup plain yogurt
1 tablespoon snipped parsley
1 tablespoon thinly sliced green onion
¼ teaspoon dried tarragon, crushed
Dash bottled hot pepper sauce

Wash artichokes, trim stems, and remove loose outer leaves. Cut off 1 inch of the tops . Snip off sharp leaf tips. Brush cut edges of leaves with lemon juice.

In a Dutch oven bring a large amount (about 3 inches) lightly salted water to boiling. Add artichokes (see photo 1, page 14). Return to boiling; reduce heat. Cook, covered, for 20 to 25 minutes or till a leaf pulls out easily. Using tongs, remove artichokes from Dutch oven. Invert to drain; cool. Spread leaves apart. Pull out center leaves and scrape out choke with a spoon; discard (see tip, page 17). Cover artichokes and chill.

Meanwhile, thaw, drain, and chop shrimp. In a small bowl combine shrimp, sour cream, yogurt, parsley, green onion, tarragon, and hot pepper sauce. Cover and chill.

Spoon *half* of the shrimp-sour-cream mixture into the center of each artichoke. Makes 2 main-dish servings.

Orange Carrots And Sprouts

2 **cups brussels sprouts** *or* **one 10-ounce package frozen brussels sprouts**
3 **medium carrots, thinly sliced (1 cup)**
1 **tablespoon butter** *or* **margarine**
2 **tablespoons orange juice**
1 **teaspoon honey**
⅛ **teaspoon ground ginger**
2 **tablespoons coarsely chopped cashews** *or* **peanuts**

Cut large brussels sprouts in half. In a medium saucepan bring about ½ cup lightly salted water to boiling. Add brussels sprouts and carrots (see photo 1, page 14). Return to boiling; reduce heat. Cook, covered, for 10 to 15 minutes or till crisp-tender (see photo 2, page 15). Drain vegetables (see photo 3, page 15). Return vegetables to the saucepan.

Meanwhile, in a small saucepan melt butter or margarine. Add orange juice, honey, and ginger. Bring to boiling. Pour over vegetables; stir gently to coat. Transfer to a serving bowl. Sprinkle with cashews or peanuts. Serves 4.

Creamy Chayote

Chayote (chah YOTE ee) is a light green, pear-shape squash with a delicate flavor.

2 **cups chopped, peeled, seeded chayote (about ¾ pound)**
½ **cup plain yogurt**
2 **tablespoons snipped parsley** *or* **1 tablespoon snipped cilantro**
½ **teaspoon sugar**
Several dashes paprika
Dash pepper
Lettuce leaves (optional)
¼ **cup chopped peanuts**

In a medium saucepan bring about ½ cup lightly salted water to boiling. Add chayote (see photo 1, page 14). Return to boiling; reduce heat. Cook, covered, about 5 minutes or till crisp-tender (see photo 2, page 15). Drain chayote (see photo 3, page 15). Chill at least 1 hour.

In a small bowl combine yogurt, parsley or cilantro, sugar, paprika, and pepper. Add chayote; toss gently. Spoon into lettuce-lined bowl, if desired. Sprinkle with peanuts. Makes 4 servings.

The Inside Scoop on Artichokes

Preparing and eating an artichoke isn't perplexing when you know what's inside.
● **Center leaves:** Purplish, prickly leaves in the middle of the artichoke. Remove these before you stuff a whole artichoke.
● **Choke:** Fuzzy, thistle portion located just below the center leaves. Scrape this out with a small, strong spoon and discard.
● **Heart:** Succulent, nut-flavored base just below the choke. Cut into bite-size pieces and dip into butter or sauce.

Taters and Toppers

If your mealtime luck is at a draw, here's an ace up your sleeve. These baked potatoes and tempting toppers will make your meal a winning hand.

Whether you're looking for satisfying South-of-the-Border Taters or intriguing Curried Chicken in Potatoes, these vegetables are worth betting on.

Potatoes with Shrimp Creole Topper

Potatoes with Shrimp Creole Topper

4 medium baking potatoes (6 to 8 ounces each)
1 8-ounce package frozen peeled and deveined shrimp
1 14½-ounce can tomatoes, cut up
¼ cup chopped onion
¼ cup chopped celery *or* green pepper
1 tablespoon snipped parsley
1 clove garlic, minced
4 teaspoons cornstarch
⅛ teaspoon ground red pepper

Scrub potatoes thoroughly (see photo 1). For soft skins, rub potatoes with shortening.* Prick potatoes with a fork (see photo 2). Bake potatoes in a 425° oven for 40 to 60 minutes or till done (see photo 3). (*Or,* bake in a 350° oven for 70 to 80 minutes.) Roll each potato gently under your hand. Cut a crisscross in the top of each potato with a knife. Press ends and push up (see photo 4).

Meanwhile, thaw shrimp; drain. In a medium saucepan combine *undrained* tomatoes, onion, celery or green pepper, parsley, garlic, cornstarch, and red pepper. Cook and stir till thickened and bubbly. Stir in shrimp. Cover and cook 3 to 5 minutes more or till shrimp are cooked. Spoon shrimp mixture over baked potatoes. Makes 4 main-dish servings.

*****Note:** To foil-bake potatoes, prepare potatoes as above, *except* omit rubbing with shortening. Prick potatoes with a fork (see photo 2). Wrap each potato in foil. Continue as directed above.

1 Scrub the potatoes gently but thoroughly with a vegetable brush under running water. Remove sprouts. Then pat the potatoes dry with paper towels.

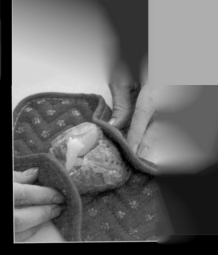

2 Prick the skin of the potatoes several times with the tines of a fork. This gives the steam a place to escape, preventing the potatoes from bursting.

3 To test the potatoes for doneness, squeeze the potatoes with a hot pad, as shown, or pierce them with a fork. When they feel soft, the potatoes are done.

4 To fluff a baked potato, gently roll the potato on the counter-top under your hand. Cut a crisscross in the top. Then, press in and up on the two ends of the potato, as shown.

Micro-Baked Potatoes

Scrub 4 medium baking potatoes (6 to 8 ounces each). Prick with a fork. In a counter-top microwave oven arrange potatoes on microwave-safe paper towels, leaving at least 1 inch between potatoes. Micro-cook, uncovered, on 100% power (HIGH) for 13 to 16 minutes or till done. (*Or,* allow 5 to 7 minutes for 1 potato; 7 to 9 minutes for 2 potatoes.) Halfway through cooking time, turn potatoes over and rearrange. Let stand for 5 minutes.

Try-a-Topper Taters

Try one of these ideas next time you top your potato.

1 medium baking potato (6 to 8 ounces)
⅓ cup sour cream dip with toasted onion *or* with bacon and horseradish

Scrub potato thoroughly (see photo 1, page 21). For soft skin, rub potato with shortening. Prick potato with a fork (see photo 2, page 21). Bake potato in a 425° oven for 40 to 60 minutes or till done (see photo 3, page 21). (*Or,* bake in a 350° oven for 70 to 80 minutes.) Roll potato gently under your hand. Cut a crisscross in the top with a knife. Press ends and push up (see photo 4, page 21). Spoon sour cream dip over potato. Makes 1 main-dish serving.

Greek Potato: Prepare potato as above, *except* substitute a mixture of ⅓ cup *plain yogurt,* 2 tablespoons sliced *ripe olives,* and a pinch of dried *oregano,* crushed, for the dip. Spoon over potato. Sprinkle with chopped tomato.

Garden Potato: Prepare potato as above, *except* substitute a mixture of ¼ cup *cottage cheese* and ¼ cup shredded *cheddar,* crumbled *feta,* or crumbled *blue cheese* (at room temperature) for the dip. Spoon over potato. Top with *alfalfa sprouts,* 1 tablespoon finely chopped *green pepper,* and 1 tablespoon finely chopped *radish.*

Low-Cal Potato: Prepare potato as above, *except* substitute *plain low-fat yogurt* for the dip. Sprinkle with snipped *chives.*

Cheesy Potato: Prepare potato as above, *except* substitute shredded *cheddar, American, Swiss,* or *Monterey Jack cheese, or* crumbled *blue cheese* (at room temperature) for the dip.

Cream Cheese Potato: Prepare potato as above, *except* substitute *soft-style cream cheese* (thinned with milk, if desired) for the dip. Sprinkle with crumbled, crisp-cooked *bacon* and sliced *green onion or* snipped *chives.*

Chili-Cheese Potatoes

Make a meal out of one of these main-dish variations.

2 medium baking potatoes (6 to 8 ounces each)
1 15-ounce can chili without beans
½ cup shredded cheddar cheese
Taco chips (optional)

Scrub potatoes thoroughly (see photo 1, page 21). For soft skins, rub potatoes with shortening. Prick potatoes with a fork (see photo 2, page 21). Bake potatoes in a 425° oven for 40 to 60 minutes or till done (see photo 3, page 21). (*Or,* bake in a 350° oven for 70 to 80 minutes.) Roll each potato gently under your hand. Cut a crisscross in the top with a knife. Press ends and push up (see photo 4, page 21).

Meanwhile, in a medium saucepan heat chili. Spoon chili over baked potatoes. Sprinkle potatoes with cheese. Serve taco chips with potatoes, if desired. Makes 2 main-dish servings.

Barbecue-Style Potatoes: Prepare potatoes as above, *except* omit the chili and cheddar cheese. In a small saucepan heat ½ cup *barbecue sauce* and ¼ cup *apple juice.* Add 2 *frankfurters,* thinly sliced; heat through. Spoon frankfurter mixture over baked potatoes. Sprinkle with ½ cup shredded *mozzarella or Monterey Jack cheese.*

Meat and Potatoes: Prepare potatoes as above, *except* omit the chili and cheese. In a medium saucepan combine 1 cup leftover *or* canned *gravy* and 1 cup cubed cooked *beef, chicken, or turkey.* Heat through. Spoon gravy mixture over baked potatoes.

South-of-the-Border Taters

One secret to great baked potato creations is to have the toppings at room temperature so the potatoes stay piping hot.

1 large tomato, peeled and finely chopped
2 tablespoons finely chopped onion
1 tablespoon finely chopped green pepper
1 tablespoon finely chopped canned green chili peppers *or* 2 teaspoons finely chopped jalapeño peppers
1 clove garlic, minced
¼ teaspoon salt
1 6-ounce container frozen avocado dip
4 medium baking potatoes (6 to 8 ounces each)

For sauce, in a medium bowl stir together tomato, onion, green pepper, chili peppers or jalapeño peppers, garlic, and salt. Cover; let stand at room temperature for 2 hours.

Meanwhile, thaw avocado dip. Scrub potatoes thoroughly (see photo 1, page 21). For soft skins, rub potatoes with shortening. Prick potatoes with a fork (see photo 2, page 21). Bake potatoes in a 425° oven for 40 to 60 minutes or till done (see photo 3, page 21). (*Or,* bake potatoes in a 350° oven for 70 to 80 minutes.) Roll each potato gently under your hand. Cut a crisscross in the top with a knife. Press ends and push up (see photo 4, page 21).

To serve, pass tomato-pepper sauce and avocado dip with baked potatoes. Makes 4 servings.

Curried Chicken In Potatoes

Use leftover chicken or turkey, or frozen diced chicken for an easy-to-make supper.

3 medium baking potatoes (6 to 8 ounces each)
1 tablespoon butter *or* margarine
¼ cup chopped green pepper *or* celery
1 tablespoon sliced green onion
1 teaspoon curry powder
1¼ cups cubed cooked chicken
1 7½-ounce can semicondensed savory cream of mushroom soup

Scrub potatoes thoroughly (see photo 1, page 21). For soft skins, rub potatoes with shortening. Prick potatoes with a fork (see photo 2, page 21). Bake potatoes in a 425° oven for 40 to 60 minutes or till done (see photo 3, page 21). (*Or,* bake in a 350° oven for 70 to 80 minutes.) Roll each potato gently under your hand. Cut a crisscross in the top with a knife. Press ends and push up (see photo 4, page 21).

Meanwhile, in a small saucepan melt butter or margarine. Add green pepper or celery, onion, and curry. Cook till vegetables are tender but not brown. Stir in chicken and semicondensed soup. Heat through. Serve chicken mixture over potatoes. Makes 3 main-dish servings.

Attention Microwave Owners!

Recipes with microwave directions were tested in countertop microwave ovens that operate on 600 to 700 watts.

Times are approximate since microwave ovens vary by manufacturer.

Scrumptious Soups

Come one, come all!
Step right up for the most
exciting selection of super-
delicious soups ever!

Main attractions include
classic French Onion Soup,
simple hearty Jambalaya
Soup, and elegant Celery-
Spinach Soup. Whatever
your pleasure—simple or
sophisticated, conventional
or classic—it's right here.

French Onion Soup

French Onion Soup

Smothered with mounds of melted cheese, this delicate soup is brimming with ooey, gooey goodness!

3 large onions, thinly sliced (about 4 cups)
¼ cup butter *or* margarine
2 cloves garlic, minced
2 14½-ounce cans beef broth
1 tablespoon Worcestershire sauce
¼ teaspoon pepper
4 ½-inch-thick slices French bread, toasted and cut into quarters
1 cup shredded Swiss *or* Gruyère cheese, (4 ounces)
2 tablespoons grated Parmesan cheese

In a large saucepan combine onions, butter or margarine, and garlic. Cover and cook over low heat, stirring occasionally, for 20 to 25 minutes or till onions are tender (see photo 1).

Stir in beef broth, Worcestershire sauce, and pepper (see photo 2). Bring to boiling; reduce heat (see photo 3). Cover and simmer for 15 minutes.

Ladle soup into 4 ovenproof soup bowls. Top each serving with 4 pieces of toasted bread (see photo 4). Sprinkle each serving with *one-fourth* of the shredded Swiss or Gruyère cheese and then *one-fourth* of the Parmesan cheese. Bake in a 500° oven for 1 to 2 minutes or till cheese is melted. Makes 4 main-dish servings.

1 Cook the onion slices in the butter or margarine until they are tender and yellowish, and their appearance changes from opaque to translucent, as shown. Don't wait for the onion slices to turn brown or they will be overdone.

2 Skip the hours of simmering once necessary for tasty soups by using canned broth for the soup base. You can substitute homemade broth, or instant bouillon granules or bouillon cubes dissolved in water if you prefer.

3 Using high heat and no lid bring the food to boiling. Boiling is the stage where many bubbles rise vigorously to the surface and break.

Lower the heat till the mixture is simmering. Simmering is the stage where only a few bubbles are formed and they burst below the surface.

4 Arrange the quarters of toasted bread atop the hot soup, overlapping the pieces slightly in the center of the dish if necessary.

The bread and cheese topping will be easier to eat when the bread has been cut into quarters rather than left in one large piece.

Oriental Chicken-Vegetable Soup

Only a few minutes of chopping plus 4 minutes of simmering and you have a fancy Oriental meal when you're ready to eat.

2   14½-ounce cans chicken broth
1   medium carrot, thinly sliced
½   cup thinly sliced or coarsely chopped, peeled daikon
1   tablespoon soy sauce
½   teaspoon grated gingerroot *or*
      ⅛ teaspoon ground ginger
1   cup cubed cooked chicken
4   ounces tofu (fresh bean curd), cut into ½-inch cubes
1   cup torn spinach
1   cup sliced fresh mushrooms
2   green onions, bias sliced

In a large saucepan combine chicken broth, carrot, daikon, soy sauce, and gingerroot or ground ginger (see photo 2, page 26). Bring to boiling; reduce heat (see photo 3, page 27). Cover and simmer for 3 minutes.

Stir in cubed chicken, tofu, spinach, mushrooms, and green onions. Return mixture to boiling; reduce heat. Cover and simmer 1 minute more or till vegetables are tender. Makes 4 main-dish servings.

Corkscrew Vegetable Soup

2   14½-ounce cans beef broth
1   cup sliced carrots
¾   cup beer
½   cup sliced celery
½   cup chopped onion
½   cup corkscrew *or* elbow macaroni
½   teaspoon dried basil, crushed
      Dash pepper
1   cup sliced fresh mushrooms

In a large saucepan combine beef broth, carrots, beer, celery, onion, corkscrew or elbow macaroni, basil, and pepper (see photo 2, page 26). Bring to boiling; reduce heat (see photo 3, page 27). Cover and simmer for 8 to 10 minutes or till macaroni is almost tender and carrots are crisp-tender (see photo 2, page 15). Stir in mushrooms. Cover and simmer 2 minutes more. Makes 6 servings.

Celery-Spinach Soup

For a favorable first impression, serve this elegant, sophisticated soup.

1   14½-ounce can chicken broth
1½ cups thinly bias-sliced celery
¼   cup chopped onion
⅛   teaspoon pepper
2   cups coarsely chopped spinach
⅓   cup dry white wine
      Grated Parmesan cheese

In a large saucepan combine chicken broth, celery, onion, and pepper (see photo 2, page 26). Bring to boiling; reduce heat (see photo 3, page 27). Cover and simmer about 10 minutes or till vegetables are tender.

Stir in spinach. Cook 2 minutes more. Stir in wine; heat through. Ladle soup into 4 soup bowls. Sprinkle generously with Parmesan cheese. Makes 4 servings.

Jambalaya Soup

Jambalaya is from jambon, the French word for ham. However, a traditional jambalaya also includes shrimp, rice, and tomatoes.

1 **pound smoked pork hocks *or* meaty ham bones**
4 **cups water**
2 **cloves garlic, minced**
1 **teaspoon dried thyme, crushed**
¼ **teaspoon ground red pepper**
1 **bay leaf**
2 **cups sliced okra (½ pound)**
1 **14½-ounce can tomatoes, cut up**
1 **cup chopped celery**
½ **cup chopped onion**
¼ **cup long grain rice**
2 **tablespoons tomato paste**
1 **8-ounce package frozen cooked shrimp**

In a large saucepan combine pork hocks or meaty ham bones, water, garlic, thyme, red pepper, and bay leaf. Bring to boiling; reduce heat (see photo 3, page 27). Cover and simmer for 45 minutes.

Remove pork hocks or ham bones. Cool slightly. Cut off meat and chop. Discard bones.

Return meat to the saucepan. Stir in okra, *undrained* tomatoes, celery, onion, *uncooked* rice, and tomato paste. Return to boiling; reduce heat. Cover and simmer about 15 minutes or till vegetables are almost tender.

Add frozen shrimp. Cover; simmer for 2 to 3 minutes more or till heated through. Remove bay leaf. Makes 6 main-dish servings.

Succotash-Squash Soup

Use any winter squash—acorn, butternut, banana, turban, or Hubbard.

1 **10¾-ounce can condensed chicken broth**
1 **soup can water (1⅓ cups)**
1 **cup fresh *or* frozen baby lima beans**
½ **cup chopped onion**
⅛ **teaspoon pepper**
2 **cups cubed, peeled, seeded winter squash**
2 **medium fresh ears of corn *or* 1½ cups frozen whole kernel corn**
Croutons (optional)

In a large saucepan combine condensed chicken broth, water, lima beans, onion, and pepper (see photo 2, page 26). Bring to boiling; reduce heat (see photo 3, page 27). Cover and simmer for 5 minutes. Add squash. Simmer about 7 minutes more or till beans are almost tender.

Meanwhile, use a sharp knife to cut off just the kernel tips from the ears of corn, then scrape the cob with the dull edge of the knife. Add corn to soup. Return to boiling; reduce heat. Cover and simmer about 3 minutes more or till vegetables are tender. Mash vegetables with a fork to thicken soup. Ladle into soup bowls. Sprinkle with croutons, if desired. Makes 4 to 6 servings.

Quick Succotash-Squash Soup: Prepare Succotash-Squash Soup as above, *except* substitute two 10-ounce packages frozen *succotash* for lima beans and corn. Combine all ingredients in a large saucepan. Bring to boiling; reduce heat (see photo 3, page 27). Cover and simmer about 10 minutes or till vegetables are tender. Mash vegetables to thicken. Serve as above.

Under the Heat

You'll do a double take with these classy side-dish vegetables. Quick as a wink, these vegetables will go from broiler pan to tabletop.

By being both fast and easy, this cooking method is twice as nice. So next time you're looking for double-delicious vegetables—broil.

Eggplant Pizzas

Eggplant Pizzas

1 **medium eggplant (about 1 pound)**
  Cooking oil
1 **8-ounce can pizza sauce**
1 **cup shredded mozzarella cheese**
  (4 ounces)
  Grated Parmesan cheese (optional)

Peel eggplant, if desired. Cut eggplant into ½-inch-thick slices (see photo 1). Place slices on the unheated rack of a broiler pan. Brush tops lightly with cooking oil (see photo 2).

Place eggplant 4 to 5 inches from the heat (see photo 3). Broil for 6 to 8 minutes or till lightly browned. Turn slices. Brush lightly with oil. Broil for 6 to 8 minutes more or till tender.

Spoon *1 heaping tablespoon* pizza sauce over each eggplant slice (see photo 4). Top slices with mozzarella cheese. Sprinkle with Parmesan cheese, if desired. Broil about 1 minute more or till cheese just starts to melt. Serve warm. Makes 5 or 6 servings.

2 Lightly brush the tops of the eggplant slices with cooking oil before broiling to prevent the eggplant from drying out or shriveling.

1 Slice the eggplant into even ½-inch-thick pieces. If you want, you can peel the vegetable before slicing. However, the peel adds color and helps hold the slice together when its cooked.

3 Adjust the broiler pan so the *eggplant* will be between 4 and 5 inches from the heat. Measure from the broiler unit to the top surface of the food.

Broiled Tomatoes

Serve crumb-topped tomatoes with meat loaf or fish.

2 **large tomatoes**
⅓ **cup soft bread crumbs**
3 **tablespoons snipped parsley**
2 **tablespoons grated Parmesan cheese**
¼ **teaspoon dried basil, crushed**
   Dash pepper
1 **tablespoon butter *or* margarine, melted**

Core tomatoes. Peel, if desired. Cut each tomato into ¾-inch-thick slices (see photo 1). In a small bowl combine bread crumbs, parsley, Parmesan cheese, basil, and pepper. Stir in melted butter or margarine.

Place tomato slices on the unheated rack of a broiler pan. Sprinkle crumb mixture evenly atop tomato slices. Place tomatoes 4 to 5 inches from the heat (see photo 3). Broil for 3 to 4 minutes or till heated through and crumb topping is lightly browned. Serve warm. Makes 4 servings.

4 Carefully spoon the topping onto the vegetable slices, then spread the topping to within ⅛ inch of the edge of each slice.

Vegetables From the Bakery

What's satisfying, sweet, *and* special? Fresh-from-the-oven baked goodies with the flavor of favorite vegetables.

Cakes and breads are the perfect place to use vegetables because shredded vegetables add flavor, moistness, and a natural sweetness.

Sunshine Carrot Cake

Sunshine Carrot Cake

An easy alternative to frosting a cake is to cut out a simple pattern on a sheet of paper. Place the pattern on the cake and sift powdered sugar over the top. Carefully remove the pattern to reveal a design of pure sweetness.

3	**or 4 medium carrots (½ pound)**
1⅓	**cups all-purpose flour**
1⅓	**cups sugar**
1½	**teaspoons baking powder**
¾	**teaspoon ground cinnamon**
½	**teaspoon baking soda**
3	**beaten eggs**
½	**cup cooking oil**
2	**tablespoons milk**
¾	**teaspoon finely shredded lemon peel**
	Cream Cheese Frosting (optional)
	Pecan halves (optional)
	Lemon peel twist (optional)

Grease the bottom and *halfway* up the sides of a 9x9x2-inch baking pan (see photo 1). Lightly flour the pan. Finely shred enough carrot to measure 2 cups (see photo 2). Set aside.

In a large mixing bowl stir together flour, sugar, baking powder, cinnamon, and baking soda. In another bowl beat together eggs, cooking oil, milk, and lemon peel. Stir in shredded carrot; mix well. Add carrot mixture to flour mixture; mix well (see photo 3).

Pour batter into the prepared pan. Bake in a 325° oven for 35 to 40 minutes or till a wooden toothpick inserted near the center comes out clean (see photo 4). Cool 10 minutes on a wire rack. Remove cake from pan; cool thoroughly on a wire rack. Frost with Cream Cheese Frosting and garnish with pecan halves and a lemon peel twist, if desired. Makes 9 servings.

Cream Cheese Frosting: In a small mixer bowl combine one 3-ounce package *cream cheese,* ¼ cup *butter or margarine,* and 1 teaspoon *vanilla.* Beat till light and fluffy. Gradually add 2 cups sifted *powdered sugar,* beating till smooth. Spread over cooled cake.

1 Brush shortening over the bottom and *halfway* up the sides of the pan. Greasing the pan only halfway up the sides gives cakes and breads smooth, even edges.

2 Rub the carrot across the shredder from top to bottom, applying a little pressure on the carrot. Use the smallest holes so you have fine shreds for the cakes and breads.

3 Pour the carrot mixture into the bowl containing the dry ingredients. Then stir with a spoon until the ingredients are well mixed.

Whole Wheat-Zucchini Bread

1 medium zucchini (about ½ pound)
1 cup all-purpose flour
½ cup whole wheat flour
1 teaspoon ground cinnamon
½ teaspoon baking soda
¼ teaspoon baking powder
¼ teaspoon salt
¼ teaspoon ground ginger
1 beaten egg
1 cup sugar
¼ cup cooking oil
¾ teaspoon finely shredded lemon peel
½ cup chopped walnuts

Grease the bottom and *halfway* up the sides of an 8x4x2-inch loaf pan (see photo 1). Finely shred enough unpeeled zucchini to measure 1 cup (see photo 2). Set aside.

In a large mixing bowl stir together all-purpose flour, whole wheat flour, cinnamon, baking soda, baking powder, salt, and ginger. In another bowl beat together egg, sugar, cooking oil, and lemon peel. Stir in shredded zucchini. Add zucchini mixture to flour mixture; mix well (see photo 3). Stir in walnuts.

Pour batter into the prepared pan. Bake in a 350° oven for 55 to 60 minutes or till a wooden toothpick inserted near the center comes out clean (see photo 4). Cool 10 minutes on a wire rack. Remove bread from pan; cool thoroughly on a wire rack. For a softer crust, wrap bread and store at room temperature overnight before slicing. Makes 1 loaf (12 servings).

4 Test the cake for doneness by inserting a wooden toothpick near the center. The cake is done when the toothpick has no batter clinging to it.

Steaming Along

All aboard! You'll know you're on the right track when you sample these tasty steamed vegetables.

The ancient cooking method of steaming is still chugging along today, popular as ever. That's because it's powered by steam, a gentle heat that allows the vegetables to retain their shape and freshness.

Next time you're at a crossing, trying to decide how to prepare your vegetables—steam ahead!

Sweet-Sour Cabbage

Sweet-Sour Cabbage

A surefire accompaniment for grilled bratwurst, knackwurst, or polish sausages.

1   **medium head cabbage (about 2 pounds)**
1   **large sweet red pepper *or* green pepper,**
     cut into ¾-inch pieces (about 1 cup)
⅓   **cup packed brown sugar**
1   **tablespoon cornstarch**
¼   **cup chicken broth**
¼   **cup red wine vinegar**
1   **tablespoon water**
2   **teaspoons soy sauce**
½   **teaspoon grated gingerroot *or***
     ⅛ teaspoon ground ginger
1   **clove garlic, minced**

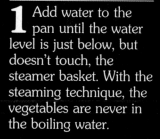

1 Add water to the pan until the water level is just below, but doesn't touch, the steamer basket. With the steaming technique, the vegetables are never in the boiling water.

2 Once the water is boiling, then lower the vegetables into the steamer basket with tongs or a large spoon.

Place steamer basket in a Dutch oven; add water to just below basket (see photo 1). Bring water to boiling. Cut cabbage into 8 wedges; remove core. Place cabbage wedges in steamer basket (see photo 2). Cover and steam for 5 minutes. Add red or green pepper (see photo 3). Cover and steam for 5 to 8 minutes more or till vegetables are crisp-tender.

Meanwhile, in a small saucepan combine brown sugar and cornstarch. Stir in chicken broth, vinegar, water, soy sauce, gingerroot or ground ginger, and garlic. Cook and stir till thickened and bubbly, then cook and stir 2 minutes more (see photo 4).

Carefully remove steamer basket from Dutch oven (see photo 5). Transfer vegetables to dinner plates or a warm serving dish. Spoon sauce over vegetables. Makes 4 servings.

3 Steam the cabbage wedges for a few minutes before adding the red or green pepper. Adding the vegetables in stages ensures that they will all be tender at the same time.

4 When the sauce becomes thick and bubbly, continue to cook and stir a few minutes longer. This fully cooks the sauce so it doesn't taste starchy.

5 Grasp the stem of the steamer basket and lift the vegetables out of the pan. Wearing an oven mitt helps protect your arm and hand from the steam.

Asparagus with Almond Sauce

1 **pound asparagus *or* one 10-ounce package frozen asparagus spears**
1 **tablespoon butter *or* margarine**
¼ **cup slivered almonds**
1 **teaspoon cornstarch**
⅓ **cup water**
2 **teaspoons lemon juice**
½ **teaspoon instant chicken bouillon granules**
   Dash pepper

Place steamer basket in a large saucepan; add water to just below basket (see photo 1, page 40). Bring water to boiling.

Wash fresh asparagus and scrape off scales, if desired. Break off woody bases at point where spears snap easily; discard bases. Place fresh or frozen asparagus in steamer basket (see photo 2, page 40). Cover and steam for 8 to 10 minutes or till crisp-tender. (Break apart frozen asparagus with a fork after 3 minutes.)

Meanwhile, make sauce. In a small saucepan melt butter or margarine. Add almonds. Cook over medium heat, stirring constantly, for 3 to 5 minutes or till golden. Stir in cornstarch. Add water, lemon juice, bouillon granules, and pepper. Cook and stir till thickened and bubbly, then cook and stir 2 minutes more (see photo 4, page 41).

Carefully remove steamer basket from pan (see photo 5, page 41). Transfer asparagus to a warm serving platter. Spoon sauce over asparagus. Makes 4 servings.

Cheesy Chokes And Leeks

Discover the nutty flavor of Jerusalem artichokes.

1 **pound Jerusalem artichokes**
¾ **cup thinly sliced leeks**
⅔ **cup milk**
2 **teaspoons cornstarch**
⅛ **teaspoon salt**
   Dash white pepper
½ **cup shredded Swiss *or* Gruyère cheese (2 ounces)**
1 **2-ounce jar pimiento, drained and chopped**

Place steamer basket in a large saucepan; add water to just below basket (see photo 1, page 40). Bring water to boiling.

Thoroughly scrub Jerusalem artichokes (see photo 1, page 21). Cut into ¼-inch-thick slices. Place Jerusalem artichokes and leeks in steamer basket (see photo 2, page 40). Cover and steam for 8 to 10 minutes or till vegetables are crisp-tender.

Meanwhile, make sauce. In a small saucepan combine milk, cornstarch, salt, and pepper. Cook and stir till thickened and bubbly, then cook and stir 2 minutes more (see photo 4, page 41). Add Swiss or Gruyère cheese and pimiento; stir over low heat till cheese is melted.

Carefully remove steamer basket from pan (see photo 5, page 41). Transfer vegetables to a warm serving dish. Pour cheese sauce over vegetables; toss gently to coat. Makes 6 servings.

Broccoli with Brie Sauce

Tastes like fondue on broccoli or cauliflower.

4 cups broccoli *or* cauliflower flowerets
   (see photo 1, page 8)
1 tablespoon butter *or* margarine
1 tablespoon all-purpose flour
⅛ teaspoon salt
   Dash white pepper
½ cup milk
2 ounces Brie cheese (rind trimmed),
   cubed
1 tablespoon dry white wine

Place steamer basket in a large saucepan; add water to just below basket (see photo 1, page 40). Bring water to boiling.

Place broccoli or cauliflower flowerets in steamer basket (see photo 2, page 40). Cover and steam 10 to 12 minutes for broccoli or 8 to 10 minutes for cauliflower or till crisp-tender.

Meanwhile, make sauce. In a small saucepan melt butter or margarine. Stir in flour, salt, and pepper. Add milk all at once. Cook and stir till thickened and bubbly, then cook and stir 1 minute more (see photo 4, page 41). Add Brie cheese; stir over low heat till melted. Stir in wine.

Carefully remove steamer basket from pan (see photo 5, page 41). Transfer broccoli or cauliflower to a warm serving bowl. Pour Brie sauce over vegetable. Makes 5 or 6 servings.

Creamed Parsnips And Peas

Imagine a slightly sweet, pale carrot and what have you got? A parsnip.

¾ pound parsnips
2 cups frozen peas
¼ cup chopped onion
2 tablespoons butter *or* margarine
4 teaspoons all-purpose flour
⅛ teaspoon salt
⅛ teaspoon white pepper
1 cup milk

Place steamer basket in a large saucepan; add water to just below basket (see photo 1, page 40). Bring water to boiling.

Wash, trim ends, and scrape or peel parsnips. Cut parsnips into ¼-inch-thick slices. Place parsnips and frozen peas in steamer basket (see photo 2, page 40). Cover and steam about 12 minutes or till vegetables are crisp-tender.

Meanwhile, make sauce. In a small saucepan cook onion in hot butter or margarine till tender but not brown. Stir in flour, salt, and pepper. Add milk all at once. Cook and stir till thickened and bubbly, then cook and stir 1 minute more (see photo 4, page 41).

Carefully remove steamer basket from pan (see photo 5, page 41). Transfer vegetables to a warm serving dish. Pour cream sauce over vegetables; stir gently to coat. Makes 6 servings.

New Potatoes with Mustard Sauce

Select your favorite mustard to flavor the sauce.

1 **pound whole tiny new potatoes (about 10 potatoes)**
2 **tablespoons finely chopped onion**
2 **tablespoons butter *or* margarine**
1 **tablespoon all-purpose flour**
¼ **teaspoon salt**
 Dash pepper
1 **cup milk**
1 **tablespoon Dijon-style mustard *or* prepared mustard**
1 **teaspoon prepared horseradish**

Place steamer basket in a large saucepan; add water to just below basket (see photo 1, page 40). Bring water to boiling.

Scrub potatoes (see photo 1, page 21). Cut any large potatoes in half. Remove a narrow strip of peel around center of each potato. Place potatoes in steamer basket (see photo 2, page 40). Cover and steam for 20 to 25 minutes or till potatoes are tender.

Meanwhile, make sauce. In a small saucepan cook onion in hot butter or margarine till tender but not brown. Stir in flour, salt, and pepper. Add milk all at once. Cook and stir till thickened and bubbly, then cook and stir 1 minute more (see photo 4, page 41). Stir in mustard and horseradish.

Carefully remove steamer basket from pan (see photo 5, page 41). Transfer potatoes to a warm serving dish. Pour mustard sauce over potatoes. Makes 4 servings.

Lemon-Basil Carrots

Here's a jewel of a sauce—so simple yet so versatile. Just vary the herb and use it on other vegetables. For starters, try thyme with broccoli, tarragon with parsnips, and garlic with beans.

6 **to 8 carrots**
2 **tablespoons butter *or* margarine**
1 **tablespoon lemon juice**
¾ **teaspoon snipped fresh basil *or* ¼ teaspoon dried basil, crushed**

Place steamer basket in a large saucepan; add water to just below basket (see photo 1, page 40). Bring water to boiling.

Wash, trim ends, and peel or scrub carrots. Thinly bias slice enough carrots to make 3 cups (see photo 2, page 8). Place carrots in steamer basket (see photo 2, page 40). Cover and steam about 15 minutes or till crisp-tender.

Meanwhile, make sauce. In a small saucepan melt butter or margarine. Stir in lemon juice and fresh or dried basil.

Carefully remove steamer basket from pan (see photo 5, page 41). Transfer carrots to a warm serving bowl. Pour sauce over carrots; stir gently to coat. Makes 4 servings.

Stuffed Specialties

Go, team, go! With an all-star lineup of squash, peppers, eggplant, and turnips, your dinnertime fans will cheer.

Everyone's a winner when you pack a savory filling into one of these vegetables. Putting it all together into one scrumptious package gives these dishes a double-play advantage.

From the first forkful to the last bite, these stuffed vegetables are real crowd-pleasers.

Curried Sausage-
Stuffed Squash

Curried Sausage-Stuffed Squash

  2 **medium acorn squash**
       (about 1½ pounds each)
1¼ **cups water**
  ½ **cup regular brown rice**
  ¼ **cup raisins**
  1 **teaspoon instant chicken bouillon**
       granules
  1 **pound bulk pork sausage**
  1 **small onion, chopped**
  ¼ **cup chutney**
  1 **teaspoon curry powder**
  ¼ **cup coarsely chopped peanuts**
       Celery leaves (optional)
       Apple wedges (optional)

Cut squash in half lengthwise. Remove seeds from squash (see photo 1). Place squash, cut side down, in a large baking pan. Bake in a 350° oven about 50 minutes or till tender.

Meanwhile, in a small saucepan combine water, brown rice, raisins, and chicken bouillon granules. Bring to boiling, then cover and reduce heat. Simmer for 40 to 50 minutes or till rice is tender and water is absorbed.

In a large skillet cook sausage and chopped onion till meat is brown and onion is tender. Drain off fat (see photo 2). Return sausage mixture to the skillet. Stir in chutney and curry powder. Cook and stir over medium heat for 2 minutes. Stir in cooked rice and ¼ cup peanuts.

Scoop out pulp from squash halves, if necessary, to make ½-inch-thick shells (see photo 3). (Reserve pulp to use as a vegetable side dish another time.) Spoon sausage mixture into squash shells (see photo 4). Bake squash, covered, for 20 to 25 minutes more.

Transfer squash to dinner plates. Garnish each with celery leaves and apple wedges, if desired. Pass sliced green onions and chopped peanuts to sprinkle atop stuffed squash, if desired. Makes 4 main-dish servings.

1 Using a sturdy tablespoon, scoop out the seeds and scrape out the strings from the cavity of each acorn squash half, as shown. Discard the seeds and strings.

2 To drain fat off the browned meat, set a colander over a grease can or disposable container. Transfer the meat mixture from the skillet into the colander and allow a few minutes to drain.

3 Scrape out just enough of the squash pulp to leave a ½-inch-thick shell, as shown. The filling is generous so some of the pulp must be removed to make room for all of the filling.

4 Return the squash shells to the baking pan, then lightly spoon the sausage filling into the cavity of each shell, piling the filling high, if necessary.

German-Style Stuffed Turnips

Sauerkraut and caraway in a Swiss cheese sauce make an ideal stuffing for turnips.

6 **large turnips (10 to 13 ounces each)**
2 **tablespoons butter *or* margarine**
1 **tablespoon all-purpose flour**
⅛ **teaspoon salt**
   Dash pepper
½ **cup milk**
¼ **cup shredded Swiss cheese**
1 **8-ounce can sauerkraut, rinsed, drained, and snipped**
¼ **teaspoon caraway seed**
   Melted butter *or* margarine
⅓ **cup crushed crispy rye crackers**
1 **tablespoon snipped parsley**

In a Dutch oven bring 3 cups lightly salted water to boiling. Peel turnips; add to Dutch oven. Return to boiling; reduce heat. Simmer, covered, about 25 minutes or till tender. Drain turnips. Scoop out pulp from turnip centers, leaving ¼- to ½-inch-thick shells (see photo 3, page 49). Finely chop enough turnip pulp to measure ½ cup; set aside. (Reserve remaining turnip pulp to use as a vegetable side dish another time.)

In a small saucepan melt *1 tablespoon* butter or margarine. Stir in flour, salt, and pepper. Add milk all at once. Cook and stir till thickened and bubbly; cook and stir 1 minute more. Add cheese; stir over low heat till melted. Stir in ½ cup chopped turnip, sauerkraut, and caraway.

Place turnip shells in a greased 12x7½x2-inch baking dish. Spoon filling into turnip shells (see photo 4, page 49). Brush with melted butter or margarine. Bake, covered, in a 350° oven for 15 to 20 minutes or till heated through.

Meanwhile, in a small saucepan melt remaining 1 tablespoon butter or margarine; stir in crushed crackers and parsley. Sprinkle cracker mixture atop turnips. Bake, uncovered, 5 minutes more. Makes 6 servings.

Orzo- and Feta-Stuffed Pepper Shells

Shop for orzo, also called rosamarina, in the pasta section of your supermarket. Look for a tiny pasta that resembles grains of rice.

⅓ **cup orzo *or* small shell macaroni**
2 **large green peppers**
1 **tablespoon butter *or* margarine**
1 **clove garlic, minced**
1 **tablespoon all-purpose flour**
½ **cup milk**
½ **cup crumbled feta *or* blue cheese (2 ounces)**
1 **small tomato, seeded and chopped (about ½ cup)**
3 **tablespoons snipped parsley**
2 **tablespoons sliced green onion**
½ **teaspoon dried basil, crushed**
¼ **teaspoon salt**
   Dash pepper

Cook orzo or small shell macaroni in boiling lightly salted water, allowing 5 to 8 minutes for orzo or 8 to 9 minutes for macaroni. Drain well.

Meanwhile, lengthwise cut green peppers in half. Remove stems, seeds, and membranes (see photo 1, page 48). In a large saucepan cook green peppers, covered, in a large amount of boiling water for 3 minutes. Drain peppers; invert on paper towels.

For filling, in a small saucepan melt butter or margarine. Add garlic and cook 1 minute; stir in flour. Add milk all at once. Cook and stir till thickened and bubbly. Stir in feta or blue cheese; remove from heat. Stir in orzo or macaroni, tomato, parsley, onion, basil, salt, and pepper.

Place green pepper shells in an 8x8x2-inch baking dish. Spoon filling into shells (see photo 4, page 49). Bake, covered, in a 350° oven for 20 to 25 minutes or till heated through. Serves 4.

Crab- and Avocado-Stuffed Zucchini

Impressing your friends with an elegant luncheon is easy when you serve this make-ahead entrée.

1   **6-ounce package frozen crab meat**
     or 6 ounces frozen salad-style
     crab-flavored fish
3   **medium zucchini (about 6 ounces each)**
1   **small avocado, halved, seeded,**
     and peeled
¼   **teaspoon finely shredded lemon peel**
1   **tablespoon lemon juice**
⅓   **cup thinly sliced celery**
1   **tablespoon thinly sliced green onion**
3   **tablespoons mayonnaise or salad**
     dressing
¼   **teaspoon onion salt**
¼   **teaspoon dried dillweed**
     Dash pepper

Thaw crab meat or crab-flavored fish; drain well. Cut zucchini in half lengthwise. With a paring knife make a cut around each zucchini half about ¼ inch from the outside edge. Then scoop out pulp, leaving a ¼-inch-thick shell (see photo 3, page 49). Chop enough pulp to measure ½ cup; set aside. (Reserve remaining pulp to use as a vegetable side dish another time.)

Place halved zucchini, cut side down, in a 12-inch skillet. Add ½ cup water. Cover and simmer for 3 to 5 minutes or till zucchini are tender. Drain zucchini; cover and chill thoroughly.

Meanwhile, cut crab meat or crab-flavored fish into bite-size pieces. Cube avocado. In a medium mixing bowl combine avocado, lemon peel, and lemon juice; toss gently. Add ½ cup chopped zucchini, crab meat or crab-flavored fish, celery, and green onion; toss to combine. In a small mixing bowl stir together mayonnaise or salad dressing, onion salt, dillweed, and pepper. Add to avocado-crab mixture. Stir gently to coat. Cover and chill.

To serve, stir crab filling. Spoon filling into zucchini shells, mounding as necessary (see photo 4, page 49). Makes 3 main-dish servings.

Savory Stuffed Eggplant

Add a crisp tossed salad and dinner's ready!

2   **medium eggplants (about 1 pound each)**
¾   **pound ground lamb or beef**
1   **medium onion, chopped (½ cup)**
1   **clove garlic, minced**
1   **7½-ounce can tomatoes, cut up**
1   **large carrot, shredded**
½   **cup chopped green pepper**
⅓   **cup quick-cooking couscous**
¼   **cup snipped parsley**
2   **tablespoons water**
1   **teaspoon dried oregano, crushed**
¾   **teaspoon salt**
¼   **teaspoon pepper**
½   **cup shredded mozzarella cheese**
     (2 ounces)
⅓   **cup grated Parmesan cheese**
2   **well-beaten eggs**

Cut eggplants in half lengthwise. Scoop out pulp, leaving ½-inch-thick shells (see photo 3, page 49). Chop pulp; set aside. Place shells, cut side down, in a 12-inch skillet; add water to skillet to a depth of 1 inch. Bring to boiling. Simmer, covered, for 3 to 5 minutes or till just tender. Drain shells; set aside.

In the same skillet cook lamb or beef, onion, and garlic till meat is brown and onion is tender. Drain off fat (see photo 2, page 48). Return meat mixture to the skillet. Add chopped eggplant, *undrained* tomatoes, carrot, green pepper, *uncooked* couscous, parsley, water, oregano, salt, and pepper. Bring to boiling; reduce heat. Simmer, covered, for 10 minutes. Remove from heat. Stir in mozzarella cheese, *half* of the Parmesan cheese, and beaten eggs.

Place eggplant shells in a 13x9x2-inch baking pan. Spoon meat mixture into shells (see photo 4, page 49). Bake, covered, in a 350° oven for 20 minutes. Sprinkle with remaining Parmesan cheese. Bake 5 minutes more. Makes 4 main-dish servings.

Microwave Magic

Abracadabra! With a push of a button and a wave of a wooden spoon, you and your ardent assistant can make vegetable dishes appear before your very eyes. Your assistant? The microwave oven, of course.

The microwave's speed and efficiency trim cooking times without wasting energy. So, when you're ready to add magic to mealtime, call on your microwave oven.

Spaghetti Squash with Tomato-Dill Sauce

Spaghetti Squash with Tomato-Dill Sauce

Great news for waist watchers—spaghetti squash makes a delicious, low-calorie alternative to pasta!

1	**medium spaghetti squash (about 3 pounds)**
2	**tablespoons water**
¼	**cup chopped onion**
1	**tablespoon butter *or* margarine**
1½	**teaspoons snipped fresh dillweed *or* ½ teaspoon dried dillweed**
1	**tablespoon cornstarch**
1	**7½-ounce can tomatoes, cut up**
3	**tablespoons chili sauce**
	Parsley sprigs (optional)

Cut spaghetti squash in half lengthwise. (Reserve 1 squash half for another use.*) Remove seeds from remaining squash half (see photo 1, page 48). Place squash, cut side down, in a microwave-safe baking dish.

Add water (see photo 1). Cover (see photo 2). Micro-cook on 100% power (HIGH) for 10 to 14 minutes or till pulp can just be pierced with a fork, giving dish a half-turn twice (see photo 3). Let stand 10 minutes.

Meanwhile, make sauce. In a small microwave-safe bowl combine onion, butter or margarine, and dillweed. Cook, uncovered, on high for 2 minutes. Stir in cornstarch. Stir in *undrained* tomatoes and chili sauce. Cook, uncovered, on high for 2 to 3 minutes or till thickened and bubbly, stirring after every minute.

Use a fork to shred and separate squash pulp into strands (see photo 4). Arrange shredded squash in a ring shape on a serving plate. Spoon sauce atop squash. Place parsley sprigs in center of ring, if desired. Makes 4 servings.

*****Note:** Place reserved squash half in an airtight container or clear plastic bag; seal. Store in the refrigerator for up to 3 days. Micro-cook according to the directions above and serve as a buttered side-dish vegetable or with warm spaghetti sauce.

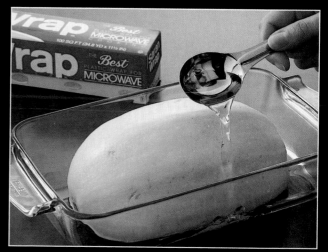

1 Adding water to vegetables creates steam during the micro-cooking. The steam helps the vegetable cook faster and more evenly.

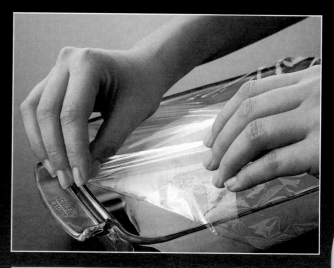

2 Substitute a covering of microwave-safe clear plastic wrap when a dish does not have a lid. Create a small vent for the steam to escape by folding back one of the corners of the plastic wrap.

3 When it is not possible to stir a food, just turn the dish around. This gives the food a different pattern of microwaves to help it cook more evenly.

4 Twist the fork slightly and the pulp of the cooked spaghetti squash will easily separate into spaghettilike strands. Then rake the squash strands out of the shell.

Wilted Spinach Salad

Wilt the spinach just before serving the meal so you can eat the salad immediately at its peak of flavor.

- **3** slices bacon
- **⅓** cup milk
- **1** tablespoon all-purpose flour
- **1** tablespoon prepared mustard
- **2** teaspoons sugar
  Dash pepper
- **2** tablespoons vinegar
- **12** cups torn spinach (1 to 1¼ pounds)
- **1** cup sliced fresh mushrooms
- **2** tablespoons water

Place 2 microwave-safe paper towels in a shallow microwave-safe baking dish. Arrange bacon atop paper towels; cover with another paper towel. Micro-cook on 100% power (HIGH) for 2½ to 3 minutes. Let stand a few minutes to crisp. Crumble and set aside.

For dressing, in a 1-cup glass measuring cup stir together milk, flour, mustard, sugar, and pepper. Cook, uncovered, on high about 1½ minutes or till mixture is thickened and bubbly, stirring every 30 seconds. Stir in vinegar; set aside.

Place torn spinach and mushrooms in a 3-quart microwave-safe casserole. Add water (see photo 1, page 54). Cook, covered, on high for 1½ to 2 minutes or just till spinach begins to wilt, stirring once. Drain well.

Transfer spinach mixture to a salad bowl. Pour mustard dressing over spinach; toss to coat. Sprinkle with crumbled bacon. Serve immediately. Makes 4 servings.

Harvard Beets

Can't beat these sweet beets!

- **4** medium beets (about 1¼ pounds)
- **2** tablespoons water
- **2** tablespoons vinegar
- **1** tablespoon sugar
- **1** tablespoon butter *or* margarine
- **1** teaspoon cornstarch
- **⅛** teaspoon salt

Wash beets thoroughly. Peel with a potato peeler; cut into ¼-inch-thick slices or cubes. Place beets in a 1½-quart microwave-safe casserole. Add water (see photo 1, page 54). Micro-cook, covered, on 100% power (HIGH) for 10 to 12 minutes, stirring once. Drain, reserving liquid. Set beets aside.

Add enough water to reserved cooking liquid to measure ¼ cup liquid. Return liquid to casserole. Stir in vinegar, sugar, butter or margarine, cornstarch, and salt. Cook, uncovered, on high for 3 to 4 minutes or till thickened and bubbly, stirring every minute till slightly thickened, then every 30 seconds. Stir in beets. Cook, uncovered, on high for 30 to 60 seconds more or till beets are heated through. Makes 4 servings.

Pea Pods and Summer Squash

6 ounces fresh pea pods (about 2 cups) *or* one 6-ounce package frozen pea pods
1½ cups bias-sliced yellow crookneck squash (see photo 2, page 8)
2 tablespoons chopped pimiento *or* chopped sweet red pepper
2 tablespoons water
3 tablespoons clear Italian salad dressing

Wash fresh pea pods. Make a cut across stem ends and pull off strings. Bias-slice fresh or frozen pea pods in half crosswise. Place pea pods, squash, and pimiento or red pepper in a 1-quart microwave-safe casserole. Add water (see photo 1, page 54). Micro-cook, covered, on 100% power (HIGH) for 3 to 5 minutes or till crisp-tender, stirring twice. Drain well.

Return vegetables to the casserole; stir in Italian salad dressing. Cook, uncovered, on high about 1 minute more or till heated through. Serves 4.

Honeyed Rutabagas And Apples

Honey and spice and everything nice—that's what tasty recipes are made of.

¾ pound rutabagas, peeled and cut into ½-inch cubes (about 2 cups)
2 tablespoons water
2 small apples, cored and cut into thin wedges
2 tablespoons honey
2 tablespoons butter *or* margarine
⅛ teaspoon ground cinnamon
Dash salt

Place rutabagas in a 1½-quart microwave-safe casserole. Add water (see photo 1, page 54). Micro-cook, covered, on 100% power (HIGH) for 12 to 15 minutes or till tender, stirring once. Drain well in a colander (see photo 3, page 15).

In the same casserole combine apples, honey, butter or margarine, cinnamon, and salt. Cook, covered, on high for 1 to 2 minutes or till apples are just tender, stirring once. Add rutabagas. Cook, covered, on high for 1 minute more or till heated through. Stir before serving. Serves 4.

Creole-Style Vegetables

Some like it hot, some not—you decide how much red pepper you like.

½ cup chopped onion
2 tablespoons water
1½ cups sliced okra (8 ounces)
¼ cup finely chopped celery
¼ cup finely chopped sweet red *or* green pepper
2 cloves garlic, minced
1 7½-ounce can tomatoes, cut up
1 teaspoon Worcestershire sauce
⅛ to ¼ teaspoon ground red pepper

Place chopped onion in a 1½-quart microwave-safe casserole. Add water (see photo 1, page 54). Micro-cook, covered, on 100% power (HIGH) for 1 minute. Add okra, celery, red or green pepper, and garlic. Cook, covered, on high for 5 to 6 minutes or till okra is almost tender, stirring once.

Stir in *undrained* tomatoes, Worcestershire sauce, and ground red pepper. Mix well. Cook, covered, on high for 1½ to 2½ minutes more or till heated through, stirring once. Serves 4.

Corn Relish

Duplicate the restaurants' relish trays with your own arrangement of corn relish, pickles, cold beets, pickled herring, and raw vegetable sticks.

3 **medium fresh ears of corn** *or*
    **one 10-ounce package frozen whole
        kernel corn**
2 **tablespoons water**
1 **small onion, finely chopped**
2 **tablespoons finely chopped celery**
2 **tablespoons finely chopped green
        pepper**
2 **tablespoons chopped pimiento**
¾ **teaspoon ground turmeric**
½ **teaspoon dry mustard**
⅓ **cup sugar**
⅓ **cup vinegar**
¼ **cup water**
2 **teaspoons cornstarch**
¼ **teaspoon salt**

With a sharp knife cut off kernel tips from fresh ears of corn. Place fresh or frozen corn in a 1½-quart microwave-safe casserole. Add 2 tablespoons water (see photo 1, page 54). Micro-cook, covered, on 100% power (HIGH) for 6 to 8 minutes or till corn is tender, stirring once. *Do not drain.* Add onion, celery, green pepper, pimiento, turmeric, and dry mustard.

In a small bowl stir together sugar, vinegar, ¼ cup water, cornstarch, and salt. Stir into corn mixture. Cook, uncovered, on high for 6 to 8 minutes or till thickened and bubbly, stirring every minute till slightly thickened, then every 30 seconds. Cover; chill at least 4 hours. Makes about 3 cups (12 servings).

Note: For longer storage, place in a freezer container, seal, label, and freeze up to 6 months. To use, thaw in the refrigerator.

Artichokes with Citrus Butter

Start off a dinner for two with this classy appetizer.

2 **medium artichokes (about 8 ounces
        each)**
    Lemon juice
2 **tablespoons water**
¼ **cup butter** *or* **margarine**
¼ **teaspoon finely shredded orange peel**
2 **tablespoons orange juice**
1 **tablespoon lemon juice**
    Orange slices (optional)

Wash artichokes, trim stems, and remove loose outer leaves. Cut off 1 inch of tops. Snip off sharp leaf tips. Brush cut edges of leaves with lemon juice.

Place artichokes in a 2-quart microwave-safe casserole. Add water (see photo 1, page 54). Micro-cook, covered, on 100% power (HIGH) for 6 to 9 minutes or till a leaf pulls out easily, giving dish a half-turn once (see photo 3, page 55). Remove artichokes from the casserole; invert to drain.

Place butter or margarine in a small microwave-safe bowl. Cook, uncovered, on high for 30 to 60 seconds or till melted. Stir in orange peel, orange juice, and 1 tablespoon lemon juice.

Arrange artichokes on salad plates; garnish with orange slices, if desired. Pour butter mixture into 2 small serving bowls or cups. To eat, pull off one leaf at a time and dunk into warm butter. Then, discard the fuzzy choke and eat the artichoke heart (see tip, page 17). Serves 2.

▶ *Artichokes with Citrus Butter*

Simply Smashing Vegetables

Looking for *simply smashing* vegetables? Then have a look here, mate.

Mashing makes the vegetables oh-so-creamy in texture. Any recipe here creates the perfect match with baked ham, crispy fried fish, grilled steak, or with any favorite meat.

And a more charming choice can't be found. It's a sure bet your family will enjoy these outstanding dishes.

Southern Sweet Potatoes

Southern Sweet Potatoes

**4 large sweet potatoes *or*
   yams (6 to 8 ounces each)
2 tablespoons butter *or* margarine
2 tablespoons orange juice *or* milk
1 tablespoon honey
¼ cup finely chopped pecans**

Scrub potatoes; prick with a fork. Bake in a 425° oven for 40 to 60 minutes or till done. (*Or*, bake in a 350° oven for 60 to 70 minutes.)

Cut a slice from the top of each potato; discard peel from slices. Scoop out each potato, leaving a thin shell (see photo 1). Mash potatoes (*see* photo 2). Add butter, orange juice, honey, and ¼ teaspoon *salt;* continue mashing till very smooth. If piping potatoes, cool slightly.

Place potato shells in a 10x6x2-inch baking dish. Using a decorating bag with a large star tip, pipe mashed potatoes into shells (see photo 3). (*Or*, spoon mashed potatoes into shells.) Sprinkle with nuts. Bake in a 425° oven for 10 to 15 minutes or till heated through. (*Or*, bake in a 350° oven for 15 to 20 minutes). Serves 4.

2 Potato Masher: Break up the potato pulp with a potato masher, as shown. Add the butter, liquid, and seasonings. Then, continue mashing till potatoes are fairly smooth.

Food Mill: Work potato pulp through a food mill or potato ricer. Add the butter, liquid, and seasonings. Stir with a spoon till fairly smooth.

Electric Mixer: In a mixer bowl beat the potato pulp with an electric mixer on low speed till almost smooth. Add butter, liquid, and seasonings. Continue beating till light and fluffy.

1 Use a spoon to carefully scoop out the sweet potato pulp leaving only a thin (about ¼-inch-thick) shell. Scrape gently to avoid tearing a hole in the shell.

3 To pipe the potatoes, fit a tip onto the decorating bag and fill the bag with the cooled mashed potatoes. Fold the end of the bag to close. Holding the full end of the bag in the palm of your writing hand, press gently to force the potatoes through the tip. Use your other hand to guide the tip.

Curried Cauliflower Puree

A hint of curry and a head of cauliflower are all you need for a sensational vegetable dish.

1 **small head cauliflower (about 1 pound)**
⅛ **teaspoon curry powder**

Wash and trim cauliflower. Cut into small flowerets. In a medium saucepan bring a small amount of lightly salted water to boiling. Add cauliflower. Return to boiling; reduce heat. Cook, covered, for 10 to 12 minutes or till very tender. Drain well in a colander (see photo 3, page 15).

Mash cauliflower using a potato masher or food mill till smooth* (see photo 2, page 62). Return cauliflower to the saucepan; stir in curry powder. Place over low heat; stir constantly till heated through. Spoon cauliflower into a serving bowl. Makes 6 servings.

*Note: If desired, place cauliflower in a food processor bowl or blender container. Cover; process or blend till smooth, stopping and scraping sides of bowl as necessary. Return cauliflower to saucepan; stir in curry powder. Place over low heat; stir constantly till heated through.

Whipped Rutabagas

1 **pound rutabagas**
½ **cup dairy sour cream**
2 **tablespoons butter *or* margarine**
¼ **teaspoon salt**
⅛ **teaspoon ground nutmeg**
1 **to 2 tablespoons milk**
2 **tablespoons snipped parsley**

Peel and cube rutabagas. In a medium saucepan bring 1 to 2 inches of lightly salted water to boiling. Add rutabagas. Return to boiling; reduce heat. Cook, covered, about 30 minutes or till tender. Drain well in a colander (see photo 3, page 15).

Mash rutabagas (see photo 2, page 62). Add sour cream, butter or margarine, salt, and nutmeg. Continue mashing till smooth, adding enough milk to moisten.

Return rutabaga mixture to the saucepan. Place over low heat; stir constantly till heated through. Spoon rutabaga mixture into a serving bowl. Sprinkle with snipped parsley and additional ground nutmeg, if desired. Makes 4 servings.

Mexican Potatoes

Balance this flavor-packed side dish with a simple entrée, such as broiled or baked chicken or ham.

3 **medium potatoes (about 1 pound)**
¼ **cup dairy sour cream**
¼ **cup milk**
½ **teaspoon chili powder**
¼ **teaspoon salt**
Few dashes bottled hot pepper sauce
¼ **cup canned diced green chili peppers, rinsed and drained**

Peel and quarter potatoes. In a medium saucepan bring 1 to 2 inches of lightly salted water to boiling. Add potatoes. Return to boiling; reduce heat. Cook, covered, 20 to 25 minutes or till tender. Drain.

Mash potatoes (see photo 2, page 62). Add sour cream, milk, chili powder, salt, and hot pepper sauce. Continue mashing till mixture is smooth. Return mixture to the saucepan; add chili peppers. Place over low heat; stir constantly till heated through. Spoon into a serving dish. Makes 4 servings.

Mashed Potatoes

A little whipping cream makes everyday mashed potatoes taste extra special.

3 medium potatoes (about 1 pound)
2 tablespoons whipping cream *or* milk
1 tablespoon butter *or* margarine
⅛ teaspoon salt
   Dash pepper

Peel and quarter potatoes. In a medium saucepan bring 1 to 2 inches of lightly salted water to boiling. Add potatoes. Return to boiling; reduce heat. Cook, covered, 20 to 25 minutes or till tender. Drain.

Mash potatoes (see photo 2, page 62). Add whipping cream or milk, butter or margarine, salt, and pepper. Continue mashing till smooth. Return potato mixture to saucepan. Place over low heat; stir constantly till heated through. Spoon into a serving dish. Makes 4 servings.

Volcano Potatoes: Prepare Mashed Potatoes as above, *except* double the recipe. Mound potatoes into a greased 8x1½-inch round baking dish. Make a shallow crater (about 3 inches wide) in the center of potatoes. Whip ¼ cup *whipping cream* till soft peaks form. Fold ½ cup shredded *American or cheddar cheese* into whipped cream. Spoon into the crater. Bake in a 350° oven about 20 minutes or till lightly browned. Makes 8 servings.

Oriental Turnips

Water chestnuts give just the right crunch.

1 pound turnips
2 tablespoons butter *or* margarine
1 teaspoon soy sauce
**½ of an 8-ounce can sliced water
   chestnuts, drained**
   Thinly sliced green onions (optional)

Peel and slice turnips. In a medium saucepan bring 1 to 2 inches of lightly salted water to boiling. Add turnips. Return to boiling; reduce heat. Cook, covered, 20 to 25 minutes or till turnips are tender. Drain well in a colander (see photo 3, page 15).

Mash turnips* (see photo 2, page 62). Add butter or margarine and soy sauce. Continue mashing till turnips are smooth.

Return turnip mixture to saucepan; add water chestnuts. Place over low heat; stir constantly till heated through and most of the liquid is evaporated. Spoon into a serving bowl. Sprinkle with green onions, if desired. Makes 4 servings.

***Note:** If desired, place turnips in a food processor bowl or blender container. Add butter or margarine and soy sauce. Cover; process or blend till smooth, stopping and scraping sides of bowl as necessary. Return turnip mixture to saucepan; add water chestnuts. Heat as above.

Saucy Vegetables

Make every mealtime an adventure. Begin your quest here by sampling our delicious duo of vegetables and white sauce. Each one of these recipes is a taste sensation worth exploring.

The route is easy— just start the vegetables cooking. As they cook, prepare the rich and creamy white sauce. You'll know your search has paid off at first bite!

Cheesy Brussels Sprouts and Tofu

Cheesy Brussels Sprouts and Tofu

A meatless main dish that's just right for lunch or a light supper.

2 cups brussels sprouts (about ½ pound) *or* **one 10-ounce package frozen brussels sprouts**
2 tablespoons butter *or* **margarine**
1 tablespoon all-purpose flour
⅛ teaspoon salt
Dash pepper
¾ cup milk
1 cup shredded American cheese (4 ounces)
2 tablespoons chopped pimiento
¼ teaspoon bottled hot pepper sauce
1 8-ounce package tofu (fresh bean curd), cut into ½-inch cubes
Chow mein noodles
¼ cup chopped peanuts

Trim stems, remove wilted leaves, and wash fresh brussels sprouts. Cut large sprouts in half. In a medium saucepan bring a small amount of lightly salted water to boiling. Add fresh brussels sprouts. Return to boiling; reduce heat. Cook, covered, for 13 to 15 minutes or till crisp-tender (see photo 1). Drain. (*Or,* cook frozen brussels sprouts according to package directions; drain.)

Meanwhile, make sauce. In a medium saucepan melt butter or margarine. Stir in flour, salt, and pepper (see photo 2). Add milk all at once (see photo 3). Cook and stir till thickened and bubbly, then cook and stir 1 minute more (see photo 4). Add cheese, pimiento, and hot pepper sauce; stir till cheese is melted.

Gently stir brussels sprouts and tofu into sauce. Heat through. Transfer mixture to a serving bowl. Serve over chow mein noodles. Pass peanuts to sprinkle atop each serving. Makes 4 main-dish servings.

Microwave Directions: In a 1½- or 2-quart microwave-safe casserole combine fresh or frozen brussels sprouts and 2 tablespoons *water.* Micro-cook, covered, on 100% power (HIGH) 3 to 5 minutes for fresh or 7 to 9 minutes for frozen, or till crisp-tender, stirring once. Drain. In a 4-cup glass measuring cup cook butter or margarine, uncovered, on high 30 to 60 seconds. Stir in flour, salt, and pepper (see photo 2). Add milk all at once (see photo 3). Cook, uncovered, on high 2 to 3 minutes or till thick and bubbly, stirring every minute. Stir in cheese, pimiento, and hot pepper sauce till cheese is melted. Add sauce to brussels sprouts in casserole. Gently stir in tofu. Cook, uncovered, on high about 2 minutes or till heated through, stirring mixture once. Serve as above.

1 Wait until you've added the vegetables to the boiling water, returned the water to boiling, and adjusted the heat so the water is just simmering. Then cover the pan and start timing the cooking.

2 Stir the flour into the melted butter or margarine until the mixture is well combined with no lumps. Combining the ingredients thoroughly at this point makes it easier to prevent lumps when the liquid is added.

Select a wooden spoon. The handle stays cool and makes it more comfortable to stir.

3 Adding the liquid all at once to the saucepan is better than trying to stir the liquid in a little at a time. Then, stir to distribute the flour-butter mixture evenly throughout the liquid.

4 Stir the mixture constantly in a figure-8 motion so it is evenly heated and does not stick to the bottom of the pan. If you stir too vigorously, the sauce will not be smooth and velvety.

Creamy Caraway Cabbage

Traditional flavors of a German menu—cabbage, caraway, rye, and mustard—all rolled into one dish.

4   cups shredded cabbage
2   cups sliced fresh mushrooms
¼   cup sliced green onion
1   tablespoon butter *or* margarine
1   tablespoon all-purpose flour
⅛   teaspoon pepper
½   cup milk
1   8-ounce carton dairy sour cream
2   tablespoons all-purpose flour
2   teaspoons prepared mustard
½   teaspoon caraway seed
⅓   cup crushed rye crackers (optional)

In a large saucepan bring a small amount of lightly salted water to boiling. Add cabbage, mushrooms, and onion. Return to boiling; reduce heat. Cook, covered, about 7 minutes or till crisp-tender (see photo 1, page 68). Drain; return to saucepan.

Meanwhile, make sauce. In a small saucepan melt butter or margarine. Stir in 1 tablespoon flour and pepper (see photo 2, page 69). Add milk all at once (see photo 3, page 69). Cook and stir till thickened and bubbly (see photo 4, page 69).

In a small bowl combine sour cream, 2 tablespoons flour, mustard, and caraway seed. Add to sauce in the small saucepan. Cook and stir till thickened and bubbly, then cook and stir 1 minute more. Add sour cream sauce to cabbage mixture; stir till coated. Heat through. Transfer mixture to a serving dish. Top with crushed rye crackers, if desired. Makes 4 servings.

Beer-Cheese Broccoli and Onion

The robust flavor of this beer-and-cheese sauce is also good with cauliflower, celeriac, or a combination of cauliflower and broccoli.

1   pound broccoli
1   large onion, cut into thin wedges
2   tablespoons butter *or* margarine
2   tablespoons all-purpose flour
⅛   teaspoon pepper
¾   cup milk
¾   cup shredded sharp American cheese
      (3 ounces)
¼   cup beer

Wash broccoli; remove outer leaves and tough parts of stalks. Cut off flowerets; set aside. Chop stems into 1- to 1½-inch pieces. In a medium saucepan bring a small amount of lightly salted water to boiling. Add chopped broccoli stems and onion. Return to boiling; reduce heat. Cook, covered, for 5 minutes (see photo 1, page 68). Add flowerets and cook 5 minutes more or till broccoli is crisp-tender; drain well.

Meanwhile, in a medium saucepan melt butter or margarine. Stir in flour and pepper (see photo 2, page 69). Add milk all at once (see photo 3, page 69). Cook and stir till thickened and bubbly, then cook and stir 1 minute more (see photo 4, page 69). Add cheese and beer; stir till cheese is melted. Stir in drained broccoli and onion. Heat through. Makes 6 servings.

Cauliflower Supreme

Rich and creamy, thanks to the Parmesan cheese and cream cheese.

2	cups cauliflower flowerets
1	cup sliced celery
½	cup chopped onion
½	cup chopped sweet red *or* green pepper
2	tablespoons butter *or* margarine
2	tablespoons all-purpose flour
¼	teaspoon salt
⅛	teaspoon pepper
1	cup milk
1	3-ounce package cream cheese, cut up
2	tablespoons fine dry bread crumbs
2	tablespoons grated Parmesan cheese
1	tablespoon butter *or* margarine, melted

In a medium saucepan bring a small amount of lightly salted water to boiling. Add cauliflower, celery, onion, and red or green pepper. Return to boiling; reduce heat. Cook, covered, 5 to 7 minutes or till crisp-tender (see photo 1, page 68). Drain.

Meanwhile, make sauce. In a medium saucepan melt 2 tablespoons butter or margarine. Stir in flour, salt, and pepper (see photo 2, page 69). Add milk all at once (see photo 3, page 69). Cook and stir till thick and bubbly, then cook and stir 1 minute more (see photo 4, page 69).

Add cream cheese to sauce; stir till cheese is melted. Stir in drained vegetable mixture. Heat through. In a small bowl combine bread crumbs, Parmesan cheese, and 1 tablespoon melted butter or margarine. Transfer vegetable mixture to a serving bowl. Top with bread crumb mixture. Makes 6 servings.

Swiss Cheese and Bacon Potatoes

Our Test Kitchen found red potatoes hold their shape better than other potatoes for this type of dish.

4	medium potatoes (about 1⅓ pounds)
¼	cup chopped onion
2	tablespoons butter *or* margarine
2	tablespoons all-purpose flour
⅛	teaspoon ground nutmeg
⅛	teaspoon pepper
1½	cups milk
¾	cup process Swiss cheese (3 ounces)
6	slices bacon, crisp-cooked, drained, and crumbled

Wash and peel potatoes. In a large saucepan bring a moderate amount of lightly salted water to boiling. Add whole potatoes. Return to boiling; reduce heat. Cook, covered, about 30 minutes or till tender (see photo 1, page 68). Drain and cool slightly. Cut potatoes into thin slices; return potatoes to the saucepan.

Meanwhile, make sauce. In a small saucepan cook onion in hot butter or margarine till tender but not brown. Stir in flour, nutmeg, and pepper (see photo 2, page 69). Add milk all at once (see photo 3, page 69). Cook and stir till thickened and bubbly, then cook and stir 1 minute more (see photo 4, page 69).

Add cheese to sauce; stir till cheese is melted. Add cheese sauce and *half* of the bacon to potatoes; stir gently till potatoes are coated. Heat through. Transfer mixture to a serving dish. Sprinkle with remaining bacon. Serves 6 to 8.

Classy Cream Soups

Ooh, là là! We've put a little bit of France into every soup in this chapter.

From across the ocean, we borrowed the French cooking technique of pureeing to give these soups their smooth, creamy texture.

So sit back and enjoy the taste of these rich, velvety soups. Each one is a love affair of flavors you'll want to experience firsthand. *Bon appétit!*

Chilled Spinach Soup

Chilled Spinach Soup

A cold, tangy soup starts any meal off on the right note.

1 14½-ounce can chicken broth
¼ cup chopped onion
1 clove garlic, minced
4 cups torn spinach *or* one 10-ounce
     package frozen chopped spinach
4 teaspoons cornstarch
¾ cup light cream *or* milk
1 8-ounce carton plain yogurt
   Plain yogurt (optional)
   Lemon slices, halved (optional)
   Mint leaves (optional)

In a medium saucepan combine *half* of the broth, onion, and garlic. Bring to boiling. Add torn spinach. Return to boiling; reduce heat. Cook, covered, for 3 to 5 minutes or till spinach is tender. (*Or,* if using frozen spinach, cook for 8 to 10 minutes or till tender.) *Do not drain.*

In a food processor bowl or blender container place undrained spinach mixture. Cover; process or blend till smooth (see photo 1).

In the same saucepan combine remaining chicken broth and cornstarch; add spinach mixture. Cook and stir till thickened and bubbly, then cook and stir 2 minutes more. Remove from heat. Stir in light cream or milk (see photo 2). Transfer spinach soup to a bowl. Cover and chill thoroughly.

Add yogurt to soup. Using a wire whisk or rotary beater mix thoroughly (see photo 3). Ladle into 4 soup bowls. If desired, garnish each serving with some additional yogurt; swirl lightly (see photo, pages 72–73). Garnish with lemon slices and mint leaves, if desired. Serves 4.

1 Process the spinach mixture until the entire mixture is smooth or pureed. Stop the machine occasionally and scrape the sides of the container to move the food back toward the blades.

2 Stir the light cream or milk into vegetable mixture after it is pureed. Light cream adds richness to the soup. For about 30 calories less per serving, use milk.

3 Gently stir the yogurt into the soup until the two mixtures are well mixed. A wire whisk is *especially* good for breaking up the yogurt, but a rotary beater or a spoon also works.

Autumnfest Soup

Our food editors sampled this soup on taste panel and unanimously declared it "Outstanding!"

**1   medium acorn squash
       (about 1½ pounds)
2   cups chicken broth
⅛   teaspoon salt
⅛   teaspoon ground nutmeg
       Dash pepper
1   cup light cream *or* milk**

Halve squash; remove seeds. Cut each piece in half. Place steamer basket in a large saucepan; add broth to saucepan. Bring broth to boiling; place squash in steamer basket. Cover and steam for 25 to 30 minutes or till squash can be pierced easily with a fork. Carefully remove steamer basket from saucepan (see photo 5, page 41). Reserve steaming liquid in saucepan.

Using a spoon, scoop squash pulp out of peel; discard peel. Place pulp in a food processor bowl or blender container. Cover; process or blend till smooth, adding a little of the reserved liquid as necessary (see photo 1, page 74).

Stir squash into reserved liquid in the saucepan; stir in salt, nutmeg, and pepper. Bring mixture to boiling; reduce heat. Stir in light cream or milk (see photo 2, page 74). Heat through. Serve immediately. Makes 4 servings.

Creamy Pea Soup

**2   cups peas *or* one 10-ounce package
       frozen peas
1   14½-ounce can chicken broth
1   cup chopped lettuce *or* spinach
½   cup chopped onion
½   teaspoon lemon pepper
¾   cup light cream *or* milk
       Croutons (optional)**

In a medium saucepan combine peas, broth, lettuce or spinach, onion, and lemon pepper.

Bring to boiling; reduce heat. Simmer, covered, for 10 to 15 minutes or till peas are very tender.

In a food processor bowl or blender container place *half* of the pea mixture. Cover and process or blend till smooth (see photo 1, page 74). Transfer smooth pea mixture to a mixing bowl. Repeat with remaining pea mixture.

Return pea mixtures to the saucepan. Stir in cream or milk (see photo 2, page 74). Heat through. Ladle into soup bowls. Pass croutons to sprinkle atop soup, if desired. Serves 4 to 6.

Cheesy Mushroom Soup

**¼   cup butter *or* margarine
2   cups chopped fresh mushrooms
2   tablespoons all-purpose flour
1   cup chicken broth
1   cup light cream *or* milk
½   teaspoon dried basil, crushed
1   3-ounce package cream cheese, cut up
       Sliced fresh mushrooms (optional)**

In a medium saucepan melt butter or margarine; add chopped mushrooms. Cover and cook over medium heat about 7 minutes or till tender.

In a food processor bowl or blender container place mushroom mixture and flour. Cover; process or blend till smooth (see photo 1, page 74).

Return mushroom mixture to the saucepan. Stir in broth, cream or milk, basil, and dash *pepper* (see photo 2, page 74). Cook and stir till thickened and bubbly. Cook and stir 1 minute more. Reduce heat. Add cream cheese; cook and stir till cheese is melted. Ladle into 4 soup bowls. Sprinkle with mushroom slices and snipped parsley, if desired. Makes 4 servings.

Broccoli-Cheese Soup

Here you skip the step of shredding the cheese. Instead, your food processor or blender shreds it while pureeing the soup.

2 cups cut-up broccoli *or* one 10-ounce
    package frozen cut broccoli
1 14½-ounce can chicken broth
1 clove garlic, minced
    Dash pepper
1 cup cubed process Swiss cheese
    (4 ounces)
2 tablespoons all-purpose flour
1½ cups light cream *or* milk
    Dairy sour cream (optional)

In a medium saucepan combine broccoli, chicken broth, garlic, and pepper. Bring to boiling; reduce heat. Simmer, covered, about 15 minutes or till broccoli is very tender. *Do not drain.*

In a food processor bowl or blender container place *half* of the broccoli mixture. Cover; process or blend till smooth (see photo 1, page 74). Pour mixture into a bowl. Add remaining broccoli mixture to the food processor bowl or blender. Cover; process or blend till smooth. Add cheese and flour. Cover and process or blend till smooth.

Return broccoli mixtures to the saucepan. Stir in light cream or milk (see photo 2, page 74). Cook and stir till thickened and bubbly. Cook and stir 1 minute more. Ladle soup into 4 soup bowls. Dollop with some sour cream, if desired. Makes 4 main-dish servings.

Hearty Potato Soup

Adding a little ham or clams rounds-out the flavor of the potatoes.

4 medium potatoes, peeled and chopped
1 14½-ounce can chicken broth
1 small onion, chopped
¼ teaspoon salt
¼ teaspoon dried basil, crushed
    Dash pepper
1½ cups light cream *or* milk
1 tablespoon all-purpose flour
½ cup finely chopped fully cooked ham
    or one 6½-ounce can minced clams,
    drained
½ cup shredded carrot

In a medium saucepan combine potatoes, chicken broth, onion, salt, basil, and pepper. Bring to boiling; reduce heat. Simmer, covered, for 10 to 15 minutes or till potatoes are tender. *Do not drain.*

In a food processor bowl or blender container place *half* of the potato mixture. Cover; process or blend till smooth (see photo 1, page 74).

Return potato mixture to the saucepan. Combine light cream or milk and flour; stir into potato mixture (see photo 2, page 74). Cook and stir till thickened and bubbly. Stir in ham or drained clams and shredded carrot. Cook and stir till heated through. Makes 4 main-dish servings.

Hearty Dry Bean Dishes

Q. I'm looking for a hot and hearty dish that's simple to make, yet deliciously homemade. Any ideas?

A. Yes! Fix your family a tasty bean dish—they're satisfying and easy to prepare. Just toss dry beans into a pot of water, add a couple of other ingredients, then sit back and let them cook.

Any one of these recipes will fill up your tummy and warm you right down to your toes.

Vegetarian Chili

Vegetarian Chili

A vegetable lover's dream come true—a meatless chili with a nice, hot kick!

½	cup dry red kidney beans
½	cup dry great northern *or* navy beans
1	14½-ounce can chicken broth
1	28-ounce can tomatoes, cut up
2	stalks celery, chopped (1 cup)
1	large onion, chopped (1 cup)
1	cup beer
1	4-ounce can diced green chili peppers, drained
1	tablespoon chili powder
1	tablespoon snipped parsley
1	teaspoon dried basil, crushed
1	teaspoon dried oregano, crushed
2	cloves garlic, minced
¼	teaspoon pepper
1	cup shredded American cheese (4 ounces)
½	cup unsalted peanuts, coarsely chopped, *or* sunflower nuts

Rinse dry beans. In a large saucepan combine beans and 3 cups *water* (see photo 1). Bring to boiling; reduce heat. Simmer for 2 minutes. Remove from heat. Cover; let stand 1 hour. (*Or,* soak beans in water overnight.)

Drain beans in a colander and rinse, discarding liquid (see photo 2). Return beans to the saucepan. Add chicken broth. Bring to boiling; reduce heat. Simmer, covered, about 1 hour or till beans are tender (see photo 3).

Stir in *undrained* tomatoes, celery, onion, beer, green chili peppers, chili powder, parsley, basil, oregano, garlic, and pepper. Return to boiling; reduce heat. Simmer, covered, for 45 minutes.

Uncover and simmer 15 minutes more or to desired consistency, stirring occasionally. Ladle into 4 soup bowls. Pass cheese and peanuts or sunflower nuts to sprinkle atop soup. Makes 4 main-dish servings.

1 Add the specified amount of cold water to the rinsed dry beans (usually about three times the amount of the beans).

2 Pour the soaked beans into a colander *discarding* the soaking liquid. Then rinse the beans thoroughly under running tap water.

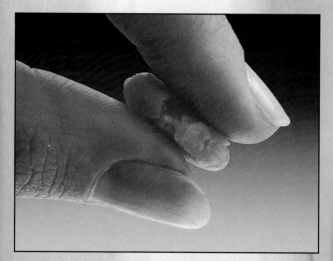

3 Remove a few beans from the saucepan and press the beans between your thumb and finger. The beans are tender when they feel soft. If there is a hard core, cook a little longer, testing them again frequently.

New England Baked Beans

1¼ cups dry navy beans *or* great
       northern beans (about ½ pound)
 ¼ cup chopped salt pork *or* 4 slices
       bacon, cut up
 1 medium onion, chopped (½ cup)
 ¼ cup molasses
 2 tablespoons brown sugar
 1 teaspoon dry mustard
 ⅛ teaspoon salt
 ⅛ teaspoon pepper

Rinse dry beans. In a large saucepan combine beans and 4 cups *water* (see photo 1, page 81). Bring to boiling; reduce heat. Simmer for 2 minutes. Remove from heat. Cover; let stand 1 hour. (*Or,* soak beans in water overnight.)

Drain beans in a colander and rinse, discarding liquid (see photo 2, page 81). Return beans to the saucepan; add 2¾ cups fresh *water* and ¼ teaspoon *salt.* Bring to boiling; reduce heat. Simmer, covered, 1¼ to 1½ hours or till beans are tender (see photo 3, page 81).

Drain beans, reserving *½ cup* liquid. In a 1½-quart casserole combine beans, reserved liquid, salt pork or bacon, onion, molasses, brown sugar, mustard, salt, and pepper.

Bake, covered, in a 300° oven for 1 hour. Bake, uncovered, for 30 minutes more or to desired consistency, stirring occasionally. Serves 6.

Overnight Soaking

Soaking dry beans overnight is quite simple. Just rinse the beans and place them in a bowl with the specified amount of cold water. Cover the bowl and set it in a cool place 6 to 8 hours or overnight.

Herbed Bean Stew

 1 cup dry navy beans
 ¾ cup dry red beans
 1 large onion, chopped (1 cup)
 2 cloves garlic, minced
 2 bay leaves
1½ cups chopped, peeled rutabaga
       or potato
 1 8-ounce can tomato sauce
 2 tablespoons all-purpose flour
1½ teaspoons instant beef bouillon
       granules
 1 teaspoon sugar
 1 teaspoon dried oregano, crushed
 1 10-ounce package frozen Italian
       green beans, thawed
 1 stick piecrust mix
 ½ cup shredded cheddar cheese
 2 tablespoons toasted wheat germ

Rinse dry beans. In a 4-quart Dutch oven combine beans and 6 cups *water* (see photo 1, page 81). Bring to boiling; reduce heat. Simmer for 2 minutes. Remove from heat. Cover; let stand 1 hour. (*Or,* soak beans in water overnight.)

Drain beans in a colander and rinse, discarding liquid (see photo 2, page 81). Return beans to the pan. Add onion, garlic, bay leaves, 4½ cups fresh *water,* and 1 teaspoon *salt.* Bring to boiling; reduce heat. Simmer, covered, 1¼ hours or till beans are tender (see photo 3, page 81).

Add rutabaga or potato; cook 20 to 30 minutes or till rutabaga is tender. Drain, reserving *1 cup* liquid. Discard bay leaves. In a 2-quart casserole combine tomato sauce, flour, bouillon granules, sugar, oregano, and ¼ teaspoon *pepper.* Add bean mixture, reserved liquid, and green beans.

In a bowl combine piecrust mix, cheese, and wheat germ. Prepare crust according to package directions; roll dough into a circle 2 inches larger than the casserole top. Place crust atop casserole; turn edge under and flute to the sides of the casserole. Cut slits in crust. Bake in a 400° oven 20 to 25 minutes or till crust is golden. Let stand 10 minutes. Makes 6 main-dish servings.

Black Beans and Rice

A tradition borrowed from the Caribbean and South American countries—black beans and rice served with a host of toppings.

1⅓   **cups dry black beans (about ½ pound)**
2   **or 3 smoked pork hocks (about 1 pound)**
1   **14½-ounce can beef broth**
1   **medium onion, chopped (½ cup)**
2   **cloves garlic, minced**
2   **bay leaves**
¼   **teaspoon pepper**
1   **tablespoon vinegar**
  Hot cooked rice
  Dairy sour cream (optional)
  Sliced green onion (optional)
  Sliced radishes (optional)
  Cooked peas (optional)
  Lime wedges (optional)

Rinse dry beans. In a large saucepan combine beans and 4 cups *water* (see photo 1, page 81). Bring to boiling; reduce heat. Simmer for 2 minutes. Remove from heat. Cover; let stand 1 hour. (*Or,* soak beans in water overnight.)

Drain beans in a colander and rinse, discarding liquid (see photo 2, page 81). Return beans to the saucepan. Add pork hocks, beef broth, onion, garlic, bay leaves, pepper, and ½ cup fresh *water.* Bring to boiling; reduce heat. Simmer, covered, about 2 hours or till beans are tender (see photo 3, page 81).

Remove and discard bay leaves. Remove pork hocks. When hocks are cool enough to handle, cut off meat and dice. Discard bones. Add diced meat and vinegar to bean mixture. Season to taste with *salt* and *pepper.* Heat through. Serve over hot cooked rice. Pass sour cream, green onion, radishes, peas, and lime wedges with beans, if desired. Makes 4 main-dish servings.

Minestrone

Jalapeño pepper in the cheese adds zing to the soup.

¾   **cup dry navy beans *or* pinto beans**
2   **10½-ounce cans condensed beef broth**
2   **bay leaves**
½   **teaspoon dried basil, crushed**
½   **teaspoon dried oregano, crushed**
2   **cloves garlic, minced**
1   **cup green beans, cut into 1-inch pieces, *or* frozen cut green beans**
1   **medium onion, chopped (½ cup)**
½   **cup diced carrots**
3   **ounces spaghetti, broken into 2-inch pieces**
½   **cup shredded Monterey Jack cheese with jalapeño peppers *or* Monterey Jack cheese (2 ounces)**

Rinse dry beans. In a 4-quart Dutch oven combine beans and 4 cups *water* (see photo 1, page 81). Bring to boiling; reduce heat. Simmer for 2 minutes. Remove from heat. Cover; let stand 1 hour. (*Or,* soak beans in water overnight.)

Drain beans in a colander and rinse, discarding liquid (see photo 2, page 81). Return beans to the Dutch oven. Add beef broth, bay leaves, basil, oregano, garlic, and 2½ cups fresh *water.* Bring to boiling; reduce heat. Simmer, covered, for 1 to 1¼ hours or till beans are tender (see photo 3, page 81).

Remove and discard bay leaves. Stir in green beans, onion, and carrots. Simmer, covered, for 10 minutes. Stir in spaghetti. Return to boiling; reduce heat. Cook, covered, 15 to 20 minutes more or till vegetables are tender. Ladle soup into 4 soup bowls. Pass cheese to sprinkle atop soup. Makes 4 main-dish servings.

Say It with A Stir-Fry

When you want the message to be great taste, let a stir-fry say it all.

With stir-frying, you always use a direct connection. The high heat quickly cooks the vegetables, letting them retain maximum flavor and freshness.

Whether it's a main dish or a side dish, the delicious delivery comes across loud and clear.

Caulifower-Asparagus Stir-Fry

Cauliflower-Asparagus Stir-Fry

¾ **pound asparagus** *or* **one 10-ounce package frozen cut asparagus, thawed**
¼ **teaspoon finely shredded orange peel**
⅓ **cup orange juice**
1 **teaspoon cornstarch**
¼ **teaspoon ground ginger**
1 **tablespoon cooking oil**
1½ **cups thinly sliced cauliflower flowerets**
2 **tablespoons sliced** *or* **slivered almonds, toasted**

Wash fresh asparagus and scrape off scales, if desired. Break off woody bases; discard. Bias-slice asparagus into 1- or 2-inch pieces. Set aside. For sauce, in a small bowl stir together orange peel, orange juice, cornstarch, ginger, and ⅛ teaspoon *salt.* Set aside.

Preheat a wok or large skillet over high heat; add oil (see photo 1). Stir-fry cauliflower in hot oil for 1 minute, then add asparagus and stir-fry about 4 minutes or till vegetables are crisp-tender (see photo 2). Push vegetables from the center of the wok or skillet (see photo 3).

Stir sauce; add to the center of the wok or skillet. Cook and stir till thickened and bubbly, then cook and stir for 30 seconds more. Stir vegetables into sauce till coated (see photo 4). Sprinkle with almonds. Makes 4 servings.

1 Drizzle the oil near the top of the hot wok, as shown. The oil coats the wok as it runs toward the center. If using a skillet add the oil, then lift and tilt to coat the cooking surface.

2 To stir-fry, use a long-handled wooden spoon or spatula to lift and turn the vegetables in a folding motion. Keep the food moving all the time for even cooking.

3 Make room to cook the sauce by pushing the vegetables away from the center of the wok or skillet.

4 When the sauce is completely cooked, stir the vegetables back toward the center of the wok or skillet. Then toss until all the vegetables are coated with the sauce.

Sweet 'n' Sour Vegetables

Crisp shredded cabbage and pea pods in an apple-flavored sweet and sour sauce.

  1   **cup fresh pea pods *or* ½ of a 6-ounce package frozen pea pods, thawed**
  ⅓   **cup apple juice**
  2   **tablespoons wine vinegar**
  1   **tablespoon brown sugar**
  1½ **teaspoons cornstarch**
  1   **tablespoon cooking oil**
  3   **cups shredded cabbage**
  2   **cups halved fresh mushrooms**

Wash fresh pea pods; cut ends and remove strings, if necessary. For sauce, in a small bowl stir together apple juice, wine vinegar, brown sugar, and cornstarch. Set aside.

Preheat a wok or large skillet over high heat; add cooking oil (see photo 1, page 86). Stir-fry cabbage in hot oil for 2 minutes (see photo 2, page 87). Add more cooking oil as necessary. Add pea pods and mushrooms. Stir-fry 2 minutes more. Push vegetables from the center of the wok or skillet (see photo 3, page 87).

Stir sauce; add to the center of the wok or skillet. Cook and stir till thickened and bubbly, then cook and stir 1 minute more. Stir vegetables into sauce till coated (see photo 4, page 87). Serve immediately. Makes 4 servings.

Curried Vegetables

An attractive array of vegetables—carrots, brussels sprouts, and red or green pepper—in a golden curry sauce.

  1   **cup brussels sprouts (about ¼ pound) *or* 1 cup frozen brussels sprouts, thawed**
  ½   **cup chicken broth**
  ¼   **cup dry white wine**
  4   **teaspoons cornstarch**
  2   **teaspoons sugar**
  2   **teaspoons curry powder**
  1   **tablespoon cooking oil**
  2   **medium carrots, bias sliced (1 cup) (see photo 2, page 8)**
  1   **medium sweet red *or* green pepper, cut into bite-size strips**
  2   **tablespoons thinly sliced green onion**
  4   **ounces tofu (fresh bean curd), cut into ½-inch cubes (about ¾ cup)**
  ½   **cup peanuts**
      Hot cooked bulgur *or* rice

Cut brussels sprouts in half. In a saucepan cook brussels sprouts in a small amount of boiling salted water for 5 minutes. Drain; set aside.

For sauce, in a small bowl stir together chicken broth, wine, cornstarch, sugar, curry powder, and ¼ teaspoon *salt*. Set mixture aside.

Preheat a wok or large skillet over high heat; add cooking oil (see photo 1, page 86). Stir-fry carrots in hot oil for 1 minute (see photo 2, page 87). Add more oil as necessary. Add brussels sprouts. Stir-fry for 3 minutes; add red or green pepper and onion. Stir-fry 1 minute more. Push vegetables from the center of the wok or skillet (see photo 3, page 87).

Stir sauce; add to the center of the wok or skillet. Cook and stir till thickened and bubbly, then cook and stir 1 minute more. Stir vegetables into sauce till coated (see photo 4, page 87). Add tofu. Cover and cook about 30 seconds or till heated through. Stir in peanuts. Serve immediately over hot cooked bulgur or rice. Makes 4 main-dish servings.

Dilled Green Beans And Tomatoes

The sour-cream-dill sauce is great with either green beans or asparagus.

¾ **pound green beans *or* asparagus**
¼ **cup water**
½ **teaspoon instant chicken bouillon granules**
½ **cup dairy sour cream**
2 **teaspoons cornstarch**
½ **teaspoon dried dillweed**
1 **tablespoon cooking oil**
1 **medium tomato, seeded and chopped**

Remove ends and strings from beans. Bias-slice beans into 1-inch pieces. Cook, covered, in a small amount of boiling lightly salted water for 4 minutes; drain well. (*Or,* wash asparagus and scrape off scales, if desired. Break off and discard woody bases. Bias-slice asparagus into 1-inch pieces.)

For sauce, in a small bowl combine water and bouillon granules; stir to dissolve. Stir in sour cream, cornstarch, and dillweed. Set aside.

Preheat a wok or large skillet over high heat; add cooking oil (see photo 1, page 86). Stir-fry green beans or asparagus in hot oil for 3 to 5 minutes or till crisp-tender (see photo 2, page 87). Push vegetables from the center of the wok or skillet (see photo 3, page 87). Reduce heat.

Add sauce to center of the wok or skillet. Cook and stir till thickened and bubbly, then cook and stir for 1 minute more. Stir in beans or asparagus. Add tomato; stir vegetables gently into sauce till coated (see photo 4, page 87). Serve immediately. Makes 6 servings.

Chayote-Rice Stir-Fry

Chilling the rice keeps it from sticking to the hot wok.

1 **tablespoon cooking oil**
2 **cups cubed, peeled, seeded chayote (about 1 medium) *or* 2 cups cubed zucchini (about 2 medium)**
1 **cup sliced fresh mushrooms**
1 **small onion, thinly sliced**
1 **small green pepper, cut into bite-size strips**
1 **clove garlic, minced**
1½ **cups cooked rice, chilled**
½ **cup fresh bean sprouts**
1 **tablespoon soy sauce**
¼ **cup shredded cheddar cheese**

Preheat a wok or large skillet over high heat; add cooking oil (see photo 1, page 86). Stir-fry cubed chayote or zucchini in hot oil for 3 to 4 minutes or till almost crisp-tender (see photo 2, page 87).

Add more oil to the wok or skillet as necessary. Add mushrooms, onion, green pepper, and garlic. Stir-fry for 3 to 4 minutes more or till all vegetables are crisp-tender. Stir in chilled rice, bean sprouts, and soy sauce. Heat through. Transfer mixture to a serving bowl; sprinkle with cheese. Serve immediately. Makes 4 to 6 servings.

Stir-Frying Without a Wok

Ready to try your hand at stir-frying, but you don't own a wok? No problem. You don't need one to stir-fry like a pro. All that's required is a large, deep skillet. The high sides on the skillet make it easy to stir and toss the foods without making a mess.

Pork and Pepper Stir-Fry

A nifty trick from our Test Kitchen—it's easier to slice very thin strips if you put the meat in the freezer for 45 minutes till it's partially frozen.

1 **pound boneless pork**
¼ **cup water**
2 **tablespoons soy sauce**
2 **teaspoons cornstarch**
¼ **teaspoon ground ginger**
  Several dashes bottled hot pepper sauce
1 **tablespoon cooking oil**
2 **medium green peppers, cut into strips**
1 **small onion, cut into thin wedges**
1 **cup halved cherry tomatoes**

Partially freeze pork. Cut pork across the grain into very thin bite-size strips. For sauce, in a small bowl stir together water, soy sauce, cornstarch, ginger, and hot pepper sauce. Set aside.

Preheat a wok or large skillet over high heat; add cooking oil (see photo 1, page 86). Stir-fry green peppers and onion in hot oil about 2 minutes or till crisp-tender (see photo 2, page 87). Remove vegetables from the wok or skillet.

Add more oil to the wok or skillet as necessary. Add *half* of the pork to the wok or skillet. Stir-fry about 3 minutes or till pork is no longer pink. Remove pork. Stir-fry remaining pork about 3 minutes. Return all pork to the wok or skillet. Push pork from the center of the wok or skillet (see photo 3, page 87).

Stir sauce; add to the center of the wok or skillet. Cook and stir till thickened and bubbly, then cook and stir 1 minute more. Return vegetables to the wok or skillet; add tomatoes. Stir pork and vegetables into sauce till coated (see photo 4, page 87). Cover and cook for 1 minute. Serve immediately. Makes 4 main-dish servings.

◀ *Cantonese Beef with Hoisin Sauce*

Cantonese Beef With Hoisin Sauce

1 **pound boneless beef sirloin steak**
¼ **cup soy sauce**
2 **tablespoons dry sherry**
2 **tablespoons hoisin sauce**
2 **teaspoons sugar**
¾ **teaspoon sesame oil**
⅛ **teaspoon whole aniseed**
1 **tablespoon cornstarch**
8 **ounces fresh pea pods (about 3 cups)**
3 **tablespoons cooking oil**
4 **cups broccoli flowerets**
3 **medium carrots, thinly bias sliced**
½ **cup sliced green onions**
½ **cup cashews**

Partially freeze beef. Cut beef across the grain into very thin bite-size strips. In a large bowl stir together soy sauce, sherry, hoisin sauce, sugar, sesame oil, and aniseed. Stir in beef strips. Cover; chill for 2 to 3 hours, stirring occasionally.

In a bowl combine cornstarch and ½ cup cold *water.* Drain beef; reserve marinade. Wash pea pods; cut ends and remove strings. Set aside.

Preheat a wok or large skillet over high heat; add *1 tablespoon* cooking oil (see photo 1, page 86). Stir-fry broccoli and carrots in hot oil for 4 minutes (see photo 2, page 87). Add pea pods and green onions; stir-fry 2 minutes more. Remove vegetables from the wok or skillet.

Add *1 tablespoon* oil. Stir-fry *half* of the beef for 2 to 3 minutes or till done. Remove beef from the wok. Add remaining oil as necessary. Stir-fry remaining beef for 2 to 3 minutes or till done. Return all beef to the wok. Push beef from the center of the wok (see photo 3, page 87).

Stir cornstarch mixture. Add cornstarch mixture and reserved marinade to the wok. Cook and stir till thickened and bubbly, then cook and stir 1 minute more. Return vegetables to the wok; stir beef and vegetables into sauce till coated (see photo 4, page 87). Heat through. Stir in cashews. Serve immediately with hot cooked rice, if desired. Makes 6 main-dish servings.

Great for Grilling

Ready to fire up for your next cookout? Make it as relaxed and lazy as a summer day.

No reason to work up a sweat trying to get meat and vegetables ready at the same time. Let things slip into place by having the vegetables share the heat with the meat.

Ever so easy, these on-the-grill vegetables make any outdoor meal a real treat.

Kohlrabi Bake

Kohlrabi Bake

*The German meaning for kohlrabi describes the flavor
—kohl means "cabbage" and rabi means "turnip."*

¾ **pound small kohlrabies**
1 **small onion, sliced**
1 **tablespoon butter** *or* **margarine**
¼ **cup chicken broth**
½ **cup shredded American** *or*
   cheddar cheese (2 ounces)
1 **tablespoon snipped parsley**

Peel kohlrabies; cut into julienne strips (see photo 3, page 9). Cut an 18-inch square of *heavy* foil (see photo 1). Place kohlrabi and onion in center of the foil. Dot with butter or margarine and sprinkle with *pepper*. Fold up foil around kohlrabi; add broth (see photo 2).

Bring up 2 opposite edges of foil and, leaving a little space for expansion of steam, seal tightly (see photo 3). Tightly seal each end.

Place foil packet on a grill directly over *medium-hot* coals (see photo 4). Grill about 30 minutes or till kohlrabi is tender. Remove from grill. Open packet; sprinkle with cheese and parsley. Serve with a slotted spoon. Makes 4 servings.

1 Measure the exact length of foil that the recipe calls for. *Heavy* foil makes a sturdy packet to hold the vegetables for grilling and is disposable for easy cleanup.

2 Shape the foil around the vegetables forming a "pan." Then pour the liquid around the vegetables.

3 Bring 2 opposite sides of the foil together and, leaving a little space for expansion of steam, fold over a ½-inch seam. Then fold the seam again once or twice and press with your fingers to seal.

4 Hold your hand, palm side down, above the coals where the food will cook. Count the seconds, "one thousand one, one thousand two, etc." If you need to withdraw your hand after 2 seconds, the coals are *hot;* after 3 seconds, they're *medium-hot;* after 4 seconds, they're *medium;* and after 5 seconds, they're *medium-slow.*

Oriental Beans

Try a duo of green beans and wax beans.

2 tablespoons soy sauce
1 tablespoon water
⅛ teaspoon ground ginger
2 cups bias-sliced green beans
   or wax beans*
½ cup sliced water chestnuts
1 tablespoon chopped pimiento

In a small bowl combine soy sauce, water, and ginger. Cut an 18x12-inch piece of *heavy* foil (see photo 1, page 94). Place green or wax beans, water chestnuts, and pimiento in center of foil. Fold up foil around bean mixture; add soy sauce mixture (see photo 2, page 95).

Bring up long sides of foil and, leaving a little space for expansion of steam, seal tightly (see photo 3, page 95). Tightly seal each end.

Place foil packet on a grill directly over *medium* coals (see photo 4, page 95). Grill for 25 to 30 minutes or till beans are crisp-tender, turning packet over once. Makes 4 servings.

*Note: If desired, substitute one 9-ounce package *frozen cut green beans* for the green or wax beans. Prepare as above, *except* grill for 20 to 25 minutes, turning packet over once.

Grilled Asparagus With Sorrel Dressing

Sorrel derives its name from the word "sour," which describes the tang of this spinachlike herb. If you want a milder flavor, substitute spinach.

¼ cup plain yogurt
¼ cup mayonnaise *or* salad dressing
¼ cup finely snipped sorrel *or* spinach
1 green onion, finely chopped
1 pound asparagus
2 tablespoons water

For sorrel dressing, in a small bowl stir together yogurt, mayonnaise or salad dressing, sorrel or spinach, and green onion. Cover and chill in the refrigerator.

Wash asparagus. Scrape off scales, if desired. Break off and discard bases. Cut an 18-inch square of *heavy* foil (see photo 1, page 94). Place asparagus in the center of the foil. Fold up foil around asparagus; add water (see photo 2, page 95).

Bring up 2 opposite edges of foil and, leaving a little space for expansion of steam, seal tightly (see photo 3, page 95). Tightly seal each end.

Place foil packet on a grill directly over *medium-hot* coals (see photo 4, page 95). Grill about 15 minutes or till asparagus is crisp-tender, turning packet over once. Serve immediately with sorrel dressing. Makes 4 servings.

Lemony Pepper Corn-on-the-Cob

3 tablespoons butter *or* margarine, softened
1 teaspoon lemon pepper
1 teaspoon lemon juice
4 fresh ears of corn
Paprika (optional)

In a small bowl stir together butter or margarine, lemon pepper, and lemon juice.

Remove husks and silk from ears of corn. Cut two 18x12-inch pieces of *heavy* foil (see photo 1, page 94). Cut each piece of foil in half to make four 12x9-inch pieces.

Place 1 ear of corn in the center of a piece of foil. Spread *one-fourth* of the butter mixture on the ear of corn. Bring up 2 long edges of foil and seal tightly (see photo 3, page 95). Tightly seal each end. Repeat with remaining ears of corn.

Place corn on a grill, directly over *medium-hot* coals (see photo 4, page 95). Grill for 20 to 25 minutes or till tender, turning often. Sprinkle corn with paprika, if desired. Makes 4 servings.

Herbed Grilled Potatoes

4 medium potatoes (about 1¼ pounds)
¼ cup butter *or* margarine, melted
2 tablespoons dry white wine
¼ teaspoon Italian seasoning

Cut potatoes *lengthwise* into quarters. In a large bowl combine melted butter or margarine, wine, and Italian seasoning. Add potatoes; toss to coat thoroughly.

Cut four 18x9-inch pieces of *heavy* foil (see photo 1, page 94). Place 4 potato quarters in the center of each piece of foil. Sprinkle potatoes with salt and pepper. Fold up foil around potatoes; drizzle with any remaining butter mixture (see photo 2, page 95).

For each packet, bring up 2 long edges of foil and, leaving a little space for expansion of steam, seal tightly (see photo 3, page 95). Tightly seal each end.

Place the foil packets on a grill directly over *medium-hot* coals (see photo 4, page 95). Grill about 25 minutes or till tender. Serves 4.

Grilled Beets

Mint jelly complements the flavor of the beets.

2 medium beets (about ¾ pound)
¼ cup mint jelly
1 tablespoon lemon juice
2 tablespoons butter *or* margarine

Wash beets; peel with a potato peeler. Thinly slice beets. In a small bowl stir together jelly and lemon juice.

Cut an 18-inch square of *heavy* foil (see photo 1, page 94). Place beets in the center of the foil. Dot with butter or margarine. Fold up foil around beets; pour jelly mixture over beets (see photo 2, page 95).

Bring up 2 opposite edges of foil and, leaving a little space for expansion of steam, seal tightly (see photo 3, page 95). Tightly seal each end.

Place foil packet on a grill directly over *medium* coals (see photo 4, page 95). Grill for 20 minutes. Turn packet over and grill 15 to 20 minutes more or till crisp-tender. Serve beets in individual bowls. Makes 2 or 3 servings.

Pan-Fried Vegetables

Planning to throw a party? Looking for something hot to really make it sizzle? Dazzle your guests with delicately pan-fried okra bites or cucumber chips.

Each vegetable is dipped in a light coating and then fried to a golden brown. The coating helps retain moistness, so they simply melt in your mouth.

You'll be the hit of the party and the talk of the town with these delicious little vegetable appetizers.

Fried Okra

Fried Okra

½ **pound okra**
2 **eggs**
 Several dashes bottled hot pepper sauce
¼ **cup cornmeal**
¼ **cup fine dry seasoned bread crumbs**
¼ **cup cooking oil**
 Salsa (optional)

Wash okra, cut off stems, and cut into ½-inch-thick slices. In a small bowl beat together eggs and hot pepper sauce. In another small bowl combine cornmeal and bread crumbs.

Stir okra slices in egg mixture to coat; drain off excess egg mixture. Then toss okra slices in cornmeal mixture (see photo 1).

In a large skillet heat cooking oil (see photo 2). Carefully add *half* of the okra to hot oil (see photo 3). Cook over medium-high heat for 2 to 3 minutes on each side or till brown (see photo 4). Drain well on paper towels. Repeat with remaining okra, adding more oil if necessary. Serve okra warm with salsa, if desired. Serves 4.

2 Pour the cooking oil into the skillet and heat over medium-high heat. Watch closely—it only takes 1 to 2 minutes to heat this small amount of oil.

3 Lower the okra slices *gently* into the hot oil with a large slotted spatula or slotted spoon. Dropping the food into the skillet can splash the hot oil on your hand and arm.

1 Dip the okra slices in the beaten egg and then toss in the cornmeal mixture, as shown. Using a fork makes quick work of this and keeps your fingers clean.

4 Turn the okra slices over when the first side is golden brown. It takes 2 to 3 minutes for each side to brown.

Fried Cucumber Chips

Dunk crispy cucumber chips in either a snappy mustard sauce or a cool dill dip.

2   medium cucumbers
1   beaten egg
¼   cup plain yogurt
2   tablespoons milk
1   cup finely crushed whole wheat
      crackers *or* shredded wheat wafers
⅓   cup cooking oil
      Sour-Cream-Dill Dip *or*
      Mustard Sauce (optional)

Peel cucumbers, if desired. Cut into ¼-inch-thick slices. In a small bowl beat egg; stir in yogurt and milk.

Dip cucumber slices into egg mixture; drain off excess egg mixture. Coat cucumber slices with finely crushed crackers or wheat wafers (see photo 1).

In a large skillet heat cooking oil (see photo 2). Carefully add *half* of the cucumber slices to hot oil (see photo 3). Cook over medium-high heat for 1 to 2 minutes on each side or till golden brown (see photo 4). Drain well on paper towels. Repeat with remaining slices, adding more oil if necessary. Serve warm with Sour-Cream-Dill Dip or Mustard Sauce, if desired. Makes 4 to 6 servings.

Sour-Cream-Dill Dip: Combine ½ cup *dairy sour cream*, 1 tablespoon thinly sliced *green onion*, ¼ teaspoon finely shredded *lemon peel*, ¼ teaspoon *Worcestershire sauce*, and ⅛ teaspoon dried *dillweed*. Stir in *milk*, if necessary, to make dipping consistency (about 1 to 2 teaspoons). Cover and chill.

Mustard Sauce: In a small bowl combine ¼ cup *plain yogurt*, ¼ cup *dairy sour cream*, and 1 tablespoon *Dijon-style mustard*. Cover and chill.

Delectable Deep-Fried Vegetables

We, the jury, find these crisp tidbits responsible for a heavenly aroma, delicious taste, and a scrumptious flavor.

As evidence, we submit an assortment of fried vegetables including the ever-popular French Fries and Cheesy Beer-Batter Onion Rings plus exciting Oriental Vegetable Tempura.

We think your verdict will be unanimous—and that you'll find yourself returning to the scene for more!

Cheesy Beer-Batter Onion Rings

Cheesy Beer-Batter Onion Rings

1 **slightly beaten egg**
¾ **cup all-purpose flour**
¾ **cup beer**
⅓ **cup grated Parmesan cheese**
1 **tablespoon cooking oil**
3 **medium mild white onions, sliced**
    ¼ inch thick (about 1 pound)
    Cooking oil *or* shortening for deep-fat
    frying

2 Use a long-handled fork to lift the onion rings out of the batter. Hold each onion ring above the bowl for a few seconds. This allows the excess batter to drip away.

For batter, in a small bowl combine egg, flour, beer, cheese, and 1 tablespoon oil. Stir just till moistened. Separate onions into rings; pat dry with paper towels to prevent spattering.

In a heavy, deep 3-quart saucepan or deep-fat fryer heat cooking oil or shortening to 375° (see photo 1). Dip onion rings into batter; drain off excess batter (see photo 2). Carefully add 4 or 5 onion rings at a time to deep hot oil (see photo 3, page 100). Fry for 1 to 2 minutes or till golden brown, turning once (see photo 3).

Carefully remove rings from hot oil. Drain on paper towels (see photo 4). Sprinkle with salt, if desired. Keep fried rings hot in a 300° oven while frying remaining rings. Serves 6 to 8.

1 Add enough cooking oil or shortening to fill the pan about ⅓ to ½ full. Use a deep-fat frying thermometer to help you monitor the temperature. Be sure the bulb doesn't touch the pan.

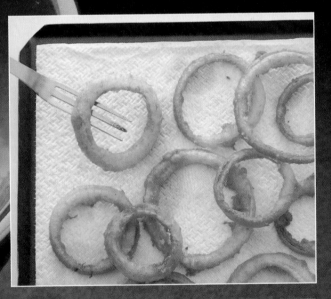

3 Use the long-handled fork to turn the onion rings over when they are golden brown on the first side, as shown.

4 Transfer the fried onion rings to a baking sheet lined with several layers of paper towels and spread them out to drain thoroughly.

Oriental Vegetable Tempura

½ **pound green beans**
½ **pound zucchini**
½ **pound fresh mushrooms**
2 **cups broccoli flowerets**
 Sweet and Sour Sauce
1 **cup all-purpose flour**
2 **tablespoons cornstarch**
¼ **teaspoon salt**
1 **beaten egg yolk**
1 **cup ice cold water**
2 **egg whites**
 **Cooking oil *or* shortening
 for deep-fat frying**

Cut green beans into 2-inch pieces. Cut zucchini into ¼-inch-thick slices; cut slices in half or quarters if large. Cut large mushrooms in half. Pat beans, zucchini, mushrooms, and broccoli dry with paper towels. Set aside. Prepare Sweet and Sour Sauce. Set aside.

For batter, in a medium bowl stir together flour, cornstarch, and salt. Make a well in the center. Combine egg yolk and ice cold water; add all at once to flour mixture. Stir just till moistened.

In a small mixer bowl beat egg whites with an electric mixer on medium speed or with a rotary beater till stiff peaks form (tips stand straight) (see photo 2, page 114). Gently fold beaten egg whites into batter. Do not allow batter to stand more than a few minutes before using.

In a heavy, deep 3-quart saucepan or deep-fat fryer heat cooking oil or shortening to 375° (see photo 1, page 104). Using a long-handled fork, dip vegetables into batter; drain off excess batter (see photo 2, page 104). Carefully add a few vegetables at a time to hot oil (see photo 3, page 100). Fry 2 to 3 minutes or till golden brown, turning once (see photo 3, page 105).

With a slotted spoon carefully remove vegetables from oil. Drain on paper towels (see photo 4, page 105). Keep fried vegetables hot in a 300° oven while frying remaining vegetables. Serve with Sweet and Sour Sauce. Serves 8.

Sweet and Sour Sauce: In a small saucepan combine ½ cup packed *brown sugar* and 1 tablespoon *cornstarch*. Stir in ⅓ cup *chicken broth,* ⅓ cup *red wine vinegar,* 1 tablespoon *soy sauce,* 1 teaspoon grated *gingerroot,* and 2 cloves *garlic,* minced. Cook and stir till thickened and bubbly. Cook and stir 2 minutes more. Serve warm or cool. Makes about 1 cup.

Calico Fritters

1 **cup packaged biscuit mix**
1 **cup chopped fresh mushrooms**
2 **tablespoons sliced green onion**
1 **tablespoon chopped pimiento**
¼ **teaspoon celery seed**
1 **beaten egg yolk**
¼ **cup dairy sour cream**
1 **egg white**
 **Cooking oil *or* shortening
 for deep-fat frying**

In a medium bowl combine biscuit mix, mushrooms, onion, pimiento, and celery seed. In a small bowl stir together egg yolk and sour cream; stir into mushroom mixture just till moistened. Set aside.

In a small mixer bowl beat egg white with a rotary beater till stiff peaks form (tips stand straight) (see photo 2, page 114). Gently fold beaten egg white into mushroom mixture.

In a heavy, deep 3-quart saucepan or deep-fat fryer heat cooking oil or shortening to 375° (see photo 1, page 104). Carefully add a few fritters at a time to hot oil by pushing mushroom mixture from a tablespoon into hot oil (see photo 3, page 100). Fry for 1 to 2 minutes or till golden brown, turning once (see photo 3, page 105).

Using a slotted spoon carefully remove fritters from hot oil. Drain on paper towels (see photo 4, page 105). Keep hot in a 300° oven while frying remaining fritters. Makes 6 servings.

French Fries

A special treat—homemade french fries, shoestring potatoes, or potato chips.

4 **medium baking potatoes**
Cooking oil *or* shortening for deep-fat frying

Peel potatoes. To prevent darkening, immerse peeled potatoes in a bowl of cold water till ready to cut. Cut potatoes lengthwise into ⅜-inch-wide strips using a knife, french-fry cutter, or crinkle cutter. Return potato strips to bowl of cold water till ready to fry.

In a heavy, deep 3-quart saucepan or deep-fat fryer heat cooking oil or shortening to 375° (see photo 1, page 104). *Thoroughly* pat pototoes dry with paper towels to prevent splattering. Carefully add a few potatoes at a time to hot oil (see photo 3, page 100). Fry for 6 to 7 minutes or till crisp and golden brown, turning once (see photo 3, page 105).

With a slotted spoon carefully remove potatoes from hot oil. Drain on paper towels (see photo 4, page 105). Sprinkle with salt, if desired. Keep fried potatoes hot in a 300° oven while frying remaining potatoes. Make 4 to 6 servings.

Shoestring Potatoes: Peel potatoes. Immerse peeled potatoes in a bowl of cold water till ready to cut. Using a sharp knife, cut potatoes into thin julienne strips (see photo 3, page 9). Return potatoes to bowl of cold water till ready to fry. Continue as directed above, *except* fry a small amount of potatoes 3 to 4 minutes.

Potato Chips: Peel potatoes. Immerse peeled potatoes in a bowl of cold water till ready to cut. Using a food processor or rotary processor, slice potatoes into thin slices. *(Or,* for very thin chips use a potato peeler to slice potatoes.) Return potatoes to bowl of cold water till ready to fry. Continue as directed above, *except* fry a small amount of thin potatoes for 4 to 5 minutes. *(Or,* fry a small amount of very thin potatoes 3 to 4 minutes).

Fried Asparagus

When fresh asparagus is at its seasonal best, serve this cheesy appetizer to a gathering of friends.

1 **slightly beaten egg**
¾ **cup milk**
½ **cup all-purpose flour**
¼ **cup cornmeal**
1 **0.7-ounce envelope Italian dry salad dressing mix**
1 **pound asparagus**
Cooking oil *or* shortening for deep-fat frying
Grated Parmesan cheese

For batter, in a medium bowl stir together egg and milk. Stir in flour, cornmeal, and dry salad dressing mix; stir till well mixed. Set aside.

Wash asparagus and scrape off scales, if desired. Break off bases at point where spears snap easily; discard bases. Cut large asparagus in half lengthwise. Cut asparagus in half crosswise. Thoroughly pat dry with paper towels.

In a heavy, deep 3-quart saucepan or deep-fat fryer heat cooking oil or shortening to 375° (see photo 1, page 104). Using a long-handled fork dip asparagus into batter; drain off excess batter (see photo 2, page 104). Carefully add 4 or 5 asparagus spears at a time to hot oil (see photo 3, page 100). Fry for 1 to 2 minutes or till golden brown, turning once (see photo 3, page 105).

With a slotted spoon carefully remove asparagus from hot oil. Drain on paper towels (see photo 4, page 105). Roll asparagus in Parmesan cheese. Keep fried asparagus hot in a 300° oven while frying remaining asparagus. Makes 12 servings.

Whole-in-One Pizza

Get your dinner in full swing with this deep-dish vegetable pizza.

Tee up this recipe with a thick, rich tomato sauce, followed by a snappy sauerkraut topping. Finish out the round with lots of gooey melted caraway cheese.

For a pizza that's right on par with any vegetable lover, sink your teeth into this one-dish delight.

German-Style Deep-Dish Pizza

1¼ cups all-purpose flour
1 package active dry yeast
½ teaspoon caraway seed
¾ cup warm water (115° to 120°)
1 tablespoon cooking oil
¾ cup rye flour
1 medium onion, chopped (½ cup)
1 small green pepper, chopped
1 clove garlic, minced
2 tablespoons olive oil *or* cooking oil
2 large tomatoes, peeled, seeded, and chopped (2 cups), *or* one 16-ounce can tomatoes, drained and chopped
1 6-ounce can tomato paste
1 teaspoon dried basil, crushed
1 teaspoon dried oregano, crushed
3 cups shredded caraway cheese (12 ounces)
1 16-ounce can sauerkraut, rinsed, well drained, and snipped
½ cup grated Parmesan cheese

For crust, in a small mixer bowl combine all-purpose flour, yeast, caraway seed, and ¾ teaspoon *salt*. Stir in water and 1 tablespoon oil. Beat with an electric mixer on low speed for 30 seconds, scraping bowl constantly. Beat on high speed for 3 minutes. Using a spoon, stir in about ½ *cup* of rye flour.

Turn dough out onto a lightly floured surface. Knead in enough remaining rye flour to make a moderately stiff dough that is smooth and elastic (6 to 8 minutes total) (see photo 1). Cover dough; let rest 10 minutes.

Grease a 14-inch deep-dish pizza pan. On a lightly floured surface, roll dough into a 16-inch circle (see photo 2). Wrap dough around rolling pin; unroll into the greased pan, extending dough 1 inch up the sides of the pan. (*Or,* if using a 15x10x1-inch baking pan, grease pan. On a lightly floured surface, roll dough into a 16x11-inch rectangle. Wrap dough around rolling pin; unroll into the greased pan, extending dough ½ inch up sides of the pan.) Cover and let rise till nearly double (30 to 45 minutes). Bake the 14-inch crust in a 375° oven for 15 to 18 minutes or till light brown. (*Or,* bake a 15x10-inch crust about 12 minutes or till light brown.)

In a saucepan cook onion, green pepper, and garlic in 2 tablespoons hot olive oil or cooking oil till onion is tender. Stir in tomatoes, tomato paste, basil, and oregano. Bring to boiling; reduce heat. Simmer, covered, for 5 minutes.

Sprinkle *1 cup* of caraway cheese over crust (see photo 3). Spread tomato mixture over crust (see photo 4). Top with sauerkraut, remaining caraway cheese, and Parmesan cheese.

Bake the 14-inch pizza about 20 minutes more or till bubbly. (*Or,* bake a 15x10-inch pizza about 15 minutes.) Makes 6 main-dish servings.

1 Knead dough by pulling the ball of dough toward you with curved fingers. Then push down and away with the heel of your hand, as shown. Turn the dough, fold it over, and repeat the process.

2 Starting at the center, roll the dough from the center to the edge. Continue rolling from the center to the edge, moving around in a circle until you have a 16-inch circle of dough.

3 Evenly sprinkle 1 cup of the cheese directly on the warm crust. This layer of cheese helps hold the pizza slices together for easy eating.

4 Gently spread the tomato mixture over the crust and first layer of cheese. Be sure to spread the mixture all the way to the edge.

So-Light Soufflés

Lights! Camera! Action! When you serve one of these showy soufflés as the star attraction, you can expect rave reviews.

The delicate flavor of vegetables costars with the light, airy texture of eggs, producing succulent soufflés that will play the lead in any meal.

Each a glamourous vegetable dish, these are soufflés you'll find worthy of a repeat performance.

Carrot Soufflé

Carrot Soufflé

4 eggs
1½ cups diced carrots *or* frozen sliced carrots
¼ cup chopped onion
¼ cup butter *or* margarine
¼ cup all-purpose flour
¼ teaspoon ground nutmeg
¾ cup milk
¼ cup dry white wine

Separate eggs (see photo 1). Set aside. In a small saucepan cook diced carrots and onions, covered, in a small amount of boiling water for 12 to 15 minutes or till tender. (*Or,* cook frozen carrots according to package directions, *except* add onion). Drain well.

In a food processor bowl or blender container place carrots and onion. Cover; process or blend till smooth (see photo 1, page 74).

In a small saucepan melt butter or margarine. Stir in flour, nutmeg, and ¼ teaspoon *salt.* Add milk all at once. Cook and stir till thickened and bubbly. Remove from heat. Stir wine into sauce.

Add egg yolks to sauce; mix till well blended. Then add carrot mixture; mix well.

Beat egg whites till stiff peaks form (see photo 2). Gradually pour carrot mixture over beaten egg whites; fold to blend. Pour into an ungreased 2-quart soufflé dish. Bake in a 350° oven for 45 to 50 minutes or till a knife inserted near the center comes out clean (see photo 3). Serve immediately. Makes 4 main-dish servings.

1 Slip the egg yolk back and forth from one shell half to the other so the egg white drains into a cup. If you get even a trace of yolk in the white, set it aside for scrambled eggs.

2 Beat the egg whites until they stand straight in stiff peaks when the beaters are lifted out, as shown. Allow about 1½ minutes to beat 4 egg whites with an electric mixer.

3 To test for doneness, insert the knife and move it slightly from side to side to enlarge the hole in the crust. Then the crust won't clean off the knife as the knife is removed.

Zucchini Soufflé

4 eggs
2 cups shredded zucchini
¼ cup butter *or* margarine
¼ cup all-purpose flour
1 teaspoon dried basil, crushed
¼ teaspoon salt
⅛ teaspoon ground red pepper
¾ cup milk
1 cup shredded cheddar cheese

Separate eggs (see photo 1). Set aside. Attach a collar to a 2-quart soufflé dish by measuring enough foil to go around the dish plus 6 inches. Fold the foil into thirds lengthwise and lightly butter one side. With buttered side in, position the foil around the dish so the foil extends 2 inches above the dish. Fold the ends of the foil till it is fastened securely. Set the dish aside.

In a small saucepan cook zucchini, covered, in a small amount of boiling water about 5 minutes or till tender. Drain well, squeezing out liquid.

In a small saucepan melt butter or margarine. Stir in flour, basil, salt, and red pepper. Add milk all at once. Cook and stir till thickened and bubbly. Remove from heat. Stir in cheese till melted; stir in zucchini. Add egg yolks; mix well.

Beat egg whites till stiff peaks form (see photo 2). Gradually pour zucchini mixture over beaten whites; fold to blend. Pour into the prepared ungreased soufflé dish. Bake in a 350° oven about 40 minutes or till a knife inserted near the center comes out clean (see photo 3). Remove collar. Serve immediately. Makes 4 main-dish servings.

Cooking Fresh Vegetables

● Timings for this chart are approximate, so use them only as a guide to cook vegetables to desired doneness.

● The maturity of a vegetable and the preparation method (whole, diced) cause some variation in timings. Cutting the vegetables into uniform pieces (for instance, halving large brussels sprouts) helps them cook more evenly.

● Except in stir-fry and microwave cooking, the amount of vegetables does not change the cooking time. For example, it takes the same amount of time to boil or steam ½ pound of asparagus as it does 1 pound. In stir-frying and microwave cooking, the cooking time depends on the amount of the vegetable (see Beans for examples).

● All timings are for the crisp-tender stage, except for those vegetables which are eaten at a tender stage. For example, potatoes and mushrooms would be tender, not crisp-tender. Other vegetables may be cooked longer to desired doneness.

COOKING GUIDELINES

Boil: Add vegetables to saucepan with a small amount of lightly salted boiling water (about ½ cup). Return to boiling; reduce heat. Simmer, covered, till done.

Steam: Place steamer basket in saucepan. Add water to just below bottom of steamer basket. Bring to boiling. Add vegetables. Steam, covered, till done.

Broil: Arrange vegetables on the unheated rack of a broiler pan. Broil 3 to 4 inches from the heat, turning once, till done.

Stir-fry: Add 1 to 2 tablespoons cooking oil to a hot wok or large skillet. Add vegetables (up to 3 cups at a time) and stir-fry till done.

Microwave: Place vegetables in a microwave-safe casserole with 2 tablespoons water (except when noted). Micro-cook, covered, on 100% power (HIGH) till done.

ARTICHOKES

Boil: In a large amount of water for 20 to 25 minutes.
Steam: 25 minutes
Microwave: One, 5 to 7 minutes; two, 7 to 10 minutes.

ASPARAGUS

Boil: Spears, 10 to 12 minutes; 1-inch cuts, 7 minutes.
Steam: Spears, 8 to 10 minutes; 1-inch cuts, 7 minutes.
Stir-fry: 1-inch bias-sliced pieces (¾ pound before trimming), 4 to 5 minutes.
Microwave: Spears (1 pound before trimming), 7 to 9 minutes; 1-inch cuts (1½ cups), 4 to 6 minutes; 1-inch cuts (3 cups), 6 to 8 minutes.

BEANS, Dry

Boil: After soaking: lima, 45 to 60 minutes; navy and great northern, 75 to 90 minutes.

BEANS, Green and Wax

Boil: 1-inch pieces, 20 to 25 minutes; French-style, 10 to 12 minutes.
Steam: 1-inch pieces, 25 to 30 minutes.
Stir-fry: After precooking 4 minutes: 1-inch pieces (½ pound, about 1½ cups), 3 minutes.
Microwave: 1-inch pieces (½ pound, about 1½ cups), 10 to 12 minutes; 1-inch pieces (1 pound, about 3 cups), 16 to 19 minutes.

BEANS, Lima

Boil: 20 to 25 minutes.
Steam: 20 to 25 minutes.

BEETS

Boil: Whole (not peeled), 35 to 50 minutes; slices or cubes, 20 minutes.
Microwave: Quarters (peeled) (1 pound), 12 to 14 minutes; slices or cubes (1 pound), 10 to 12 minutes.

BROCCOLI

Boil: Spears, 11 to 12 minutes; ½-inch cuts, 10 to 12 minutes.
Steam: Spears, 12 to 14 minutes; ½-inch cuts, 10 to 12 minutes.
Stir-fry: ½-inch cuts (½ pound), 3 to 4 minutes.
Microwave: Spears (1 pound), 6 to 9 minutes; ½-inch cuts (1 pound), 6 to 8 minutes.

BRUSSELS SPROUTS

Boil: 13 to 15 minutes.
Steam: 15 minutes.
Stir-fry: After precooking 5 minutes: whole or halves (½ pound, about 2 cups), 5 minutes.
Microwave: Whole or halves (1 pound, about 4 cups), 6 to 8 minutes; (½ pound, about 2 cups) 3 to 5 minutes.

CABBAGE

Boil: Wedges, 10 to 12 minutes; shredded, 5 to 7 minutes.
Steam: Wedges, 10 to 13 minutes; shredded, 5 to 7 minutes.
Stir-fry: Shredded (2½ cups), 3 minutes.
Microwave: Six wedges, 10 to 12 minutes; shredded (5 cups), 10 to 12 minutes.

CARROTS

Boil: Whole or strips, 15 to 20 minutes; slices, 12 to 14 minutes; shredded, 5 minutes.
Steam: Slices, 15 minutes; diced, 12 to 15 minutes.
Stir-fry: Thin slices or julienne strips (1½ cups), 4 to 5 minutes.
Microwave: Slices (2½ cups), 8 to 11 minutes.

CAULIFLOWER

Boil: Whole head, 12 to 15 minutes; flowerets, 7 to 10 minutes.
Steam: Whole head, 15 to 17 minutes; flowerets, 8 to 10 minutes.
Stir-fry: Thin slices (2 cups), 5 minutes.

CAULIFLOWER (continued)

Microwave: Whole head (1 to 1½ pounds after trimming; add ¼ cup water), 8 to 10 minutes; flowerets (3 cups), 4 to 6 minutes.

CELERIAC

Boil: Cubes, 10 minutes.
Steam: Cubes, 10 minutes.
Stir-fry: Cubes or strips (½ pound, about 1¼ cups), 3 to 5 minutes.
Microwave: Cubes (1¼ cups), 4 to 5 minutes.

CELERY

Boil: Slices, 7 minutes.
Steam: Slices, 7 minutes.
Stir-fry: Thin slices (1½ cups), 3 to 4 minutes.
Microwave: ½-inch slices (1 cup), 3 to 5 minutes; chopped (1 cup), 3 to 5 minutes.

CHAYOTE

Boil: ¾-inch cubes, 5 minutes.
Steam: ¾-inch cubes, 8 minutes.
Microwave: ¾-inch cubes (1 medium, about 1⅓ cups), 4 to 6 minutes.

CORN

Boil: On the cob, 6 to 8 minutes; kernels, 4 minutes.
Steam: On the cob, 6 to 8 minutes; kernels, 4 to 5 minutes.
Microwave: On the cob, 1 ear, 2 to 3 minutes; 2 ears, 4 to 5 minutes; 3 ears, 6 to 7 minutes; 4 ears, 8 to 9 minutes; 5 ears, 10 to 12 minutes; 6 ears, 12 to 14 minutes.
Kernels (2 cups), 5 to 6 minutes.

DAIKON

Boil: Strips, 5 minutes
Steam: Strips, 5 to 7 minutes
Stir-fry: Strips (1 cup), 2½ minutes
Microwave: Strips (1 cup), 3 to 4 minutes

Cooking Fresh
Vegetables (continued)

EGGPLANT

Boil: ¾-inch cubes, 5 to 7 minutes.
Steam: ¾-inch cubes, 8 minutes.
Broil: 1-inch slices, 10 to 12 minutes.
Stir-fry: ¾-inch cubes (4½ cups), 6 to 7 minutes.
Microwave: ¾-inch cubes (5 cups),
 4 to 6 minutes.

GREENS

Boil: Torn, 9 to 12 minutes.
Steam: Torn, 10 to 12 minutes.
Stir-fry: Torn (4 cups), 1 to 2 minutes.
Microwave: Torn (12 cups), 7 to 9 minutes.

JERUSALEM ARTICHOKE

Boil: Slices (add ¾ to 1 cup water),
 8 to 10 minutes
Steam: ¼-inch slices, 10 to 12 minutes.
Microwave: Slices (1 pound, about 2 cups), 5 to 7
 minutes

JICAMA

Boil: Cubes, 15 minutes.
Steam: Cubes, 15 minutes.
Microwave: ½-inch cubes (2 cups),
 6 to 8 minutes.

KOHLRABI

Boil: ¾-inch cubes, 8 minutes.
Steam: ¾-inch cubes, 8 minutes.
Microwave: Cubes (2½ cups), 4 to 6 minutes.

LEEKS

Boil: ½-inch slices, 10 minutes.
Steam: ½-inch slices, 10 minutes.
Stir-fry: ½-inch slices (1¼ cups), 3 to 4 minutes.
Microwave: ½-inch slices (1¼ cups),
 3 to 4 minutes.

MUSHROOMS

Boil: Whole, 10 to 12 minutes.
Steam: Whole, 10 to 12 minutes.
Broil: Whole, 10 minutes.
Stir-fry: Slices (¼ pound, 1½ cups), 1 minute.
Microwave: Slices (½ pound, 3 cups), 2½ to 3½
 minutes.

OKRA

Boil: Slices, 8 minutes.
Steam: Slices, 5 to 7 minutes.
Microwave: Slices (2 cups), 3 to 5 minutes.

ONIONS

Boil: Quarters and small whole, 25 to 30 minutes;
 slices, 10 minutes.
Steam: Slices, 10 to 12 minutes.
Stir-fry: Chopped (1 medium), 2 minutes; thin
 wedges (1 medium), 3 minutes.
Microwave: Quarters (4 medium), 6 to 8 minutes;
 slices or chopped (1 medium), 2 to 3 minutes.

PARSNIPS

Boil: Cubes, 12 to 15 minutes.
Steam: ¼-inch slices and cubes, 12 to 15 minutes.
Stir-fry: Thin slices (1½ cups), 4 to 5 minutes.
Microwave: ¼-inch slices (1½ cups),
 4 to 6 minutes.

PEAS, Green

Boil: Shelled, 10 to 12 minutes.
Steam: Shelled, 12 to 15 minutes.
Microwave: Shelled (2 cups), 6 to 8 minutes.

PEA PODS

Boil: 2 to 4 minutes.
Steam: 2 to 4 minutes.
Stir-fry: 2½ to 3 cups, 2 to 3 minutes.
Microwave: 2½ to 3 cups, 3 to 5 minutes.

PEPPERS, Green, Sweet Red, and Yellow

Boil: 3 to 5 minutes.
Steam: 5 to 8 minutes.
Stir-Fry: ¾-inch pieces (1 medium or ¾ cup), 1½ minutes.
Microwave: Chopped (1 medium or ¾ cup), 3 to 5 minutes.

POTATOES

Boil: Whole, 25 to 40 minutes; quarters, 20 to 25 minutes; tiny new, 13 to 15 minutes; diced, 12 minutes.
Steam: Quartered, 20 to 25 minutes; tiny new, 20 minutes; diced, 12 minutes.
Bake: Whole, 40 to 60 minutes at 425°; 70 to 80 minutes at 350°.
Microwave: Prick skin in several places. Whole, 1 medium, 5 to 7 minutes; 2 medium, 7 to 9 minutes; 4 medium, 13 to 16 minutes. Quarters (4 medium), 10 to 12 minutes. Cubes and slices (about 3 medium), 6 to 8. Tiny new potatoes (about 8), 6 to 8 minutes.

RUTABAGA

Boil: ½-inch cubes and ¼-inch slices, 18 to 20 minutes.
Steam: ½-inch cubes, 22 to 25 minutes; ¼-inch slices, 18 to 20 minutes.
Stir-fry: ½-inch cubes (1½ cups), 6 to 7 minutes.
Microwave: ½-inch cubes (4 cups), 11 to 13 minutes.

SPINACH

Boil: Torn, 3 to 5 minutes.
Steam: Torn, 4 minutes.
Stir-fry: Torn (4 cups), 1 to 2 minutes.
Microwave: Leaves (12 cups), 7 to 9 minutes.

SQUASH, Winter (Acorn, Butternut)

Boil: Slices, 10 minutes; cubes, 6 to 8 minutes.
Steam: Quarters, 25 to 30 minutes; slices, 7 to 8 minutes; cubes 6 to 8 minutes.

SQUASH, Winter (continued)

Bake: Halves, 30 minutes at 350° cut side down, then for 10 to 20 minutes cut side up.
Microwave: Acorn squash halves (2), 6½ to 8½ minutes; butternut squash halves (2), 10 to 13 minutes.

SQUASH, Summer (Zucchini, Yellow)

Boil: Slices, 5 to 10 minutes.
Steam: Slices, 5 to 10 minutes.
Stir-fry: ¼-inch slices (1 medium squash), 3 to 3½ minutes.
Microwave: ¼-inch slices (4 cups), 6 to 8 minutes.

SWEET POTATOES

Boil: Whole, 25 to 35 minutes; ¼-inch slices, 15 minutes.
Steam: Quarters, 12 minutes; ¼-inch slices, 15 minutes.
Bake: Whole, 40 to 45 minutes at 375°.
Stir-fry: ¼-inch slices (1½ cups), 4 to 5 minutes.
Microwave: Prick skin in several places. Whole, 4 medium (about 1 pound), 7 to 9 minutes. Cubes (3 medium, about 1 pound), 6 to 8 minutes.

TOMATOES

Boil: Slices and cubes, 10 to 12 minutes.
Broil: ½-inch slices, 3 to 4 minutes.
Stir-fry: 1 minute to heat through.
Microwave: ¼-inch slices (4 medium), 3 to 5 minutes.

TURNIPS

Boil: ½-inch cubes and ¼-inch slices, 10 to 15 minutes.
Steam: Cubes, 20 to 25 minutes.
Stir-fry: ½-inch cubes (1½ cups), 3½ to 4½ minutes.
Microwave: ½-inch cubes (2 cups), 10 to 12 minutes.

Kohlrabi

Leek

Jicama

Okra

Unusual Vegetables

Supermarket produce sections look like works of art with the beautiful array of fresh vegetables now available. And, no doubt, some of these vegetables will be new to you.

This guide acquaints you with a few of these unusual vegetables. It lets you select and prepare each like an expert. Check the index for recipes using these vegetables.

Kohlrabi

It may look like a bulb, but kohlrabi is actually a stem vegetable that has the flavors of cabbage and turnips combined. It can be green, lavender, or white in color.

Choose small kohlrabi, about the size of a tennis ball or smaller, for a mild flavor and crisp texture.

To use kohlrabi, cut off any leaves or stalk and rinse. Peel it before or after cooking. Or, peel it to use raw in salads and on relish trays as you would celery or turnips. The leaves of kohlrabi also can be cooked like spinach.

Leek

Leeks look like a gigantic green onion but have a milder, sweeter flavor than onions. When selecting them, choose leeks with a long white base, not those that have a bulb like green onions. Choose small to medium-size leeks with fresh green leaves.

Wait until you're ready to use the leeks to wash them. Cut off the roots and tough outer leaves. Split the leek in half lengthwise and swish it in water. Then rinse it thoroughly under running water to remove all the sand.

Use leeks as you would onions—either raw or cooked till crisp-tender. Leeks also make attractive garnishes.

Chayote

Jerusalem Artichoke

Daikon

Jicama

Jicama (HEE kuh muh), a root vegetable, is a staple in Mexico, just as potatoes are in the United States. It's crisp with a mild, sweet flavor.

Purchase a firm jicama with no mold. Store in a cool, dark place or in the refrigerator. When you're ready to use the jicama, peel off the skin and fibrous outer layer with a knife. Slice or dice it to use raw in salads and on relish trays. Or, try cooking them as you would cook potatoes.

Okra

These small green pods are a favorite of Southern cooks. Their natural thickening is a must in classic Cajun gumbo. Favorite ways of using okra include batter-frying, pickling, and stewing with tomatoes.

Choose small, crisp okra, and avoid large, woody ones or any that are turning black. Use the okra within a few days or freeze it for extended storage.

Daikon

Daikon (DIKE un) is a long, white Japanese radish sometimes called mooli or muli. It's common in Oriental cookery—in stir-frys, as pickles (Takuan), or with raw fish. Daikon's peppery flavor is similar to a hot radish.

Choose firm, smooth, daikon with no cracks or wilted leaves. Cut off any leaves and store it in the refrigerator for a few days. Peel it with a vegetable peeler and grate or slice it. Daikon is served raw as a relish, cooked like turnips in soups, or stir-fried.

Chayote

Chayote (chah YOTE ee), a pear-shape squash, is also called mirliton or mango squash. It tastes like apples and cucumbers and its texture is similar to cucumbers.

When purchasing chayote, look for small, firm, unblemished ones. They can be boiled, baked, or steamed, either peeled or unpeeled. Chayote can be substituted for squash in salads, soups, and desserts.

Jerusalem Artichoke

A native of North America and no relation to the familiar globe artichoke, these small tubers are also called sunchokes. When eaten raw, they have a sweet, nutty flavor and crunchy texture. When Jerusalem artichokes are cooked, their flavor is similar to globe artichokes.

Use Jerusalem artichokes raw in salads and with dips. Or, cook them like potatoes. Leave the peel on to cook and then peel, if desired.

Nutrition Analysis Chart

Use these analyses to compare nutritional values of different recipes. This information was calculated using Agriculture Handbook Number 8, published by the United States Department of Agriculture, as the primary source.

In compiling the nutrition analyses, we made the following assumptions:
● For all of the main-dish meat recipes, the nutrition analyses were calculated using measurements for cooked meat.

● Garnishes and optional ingredients were not included in the nutrition analyses.
● If a marinade was brushed over a food during cooking, the analysis includes all of the marinade.
● When two ingredient options appear in a recipe, calculations were made using the first one.
● For ingredients of variable weight (such as "2½- to 3-pound broiler-fryer chicken") or for recipes with a serving range ("Makes 4 to 6 servings"), calculations were made using the first figure.

	Per Serving						Percent U.S. RDA Per Serving							
	Calories	Protein (g)	Carbohydrate (g)	Fat (g)	Sodium (mg)	Potassium (mg)	Protein	Vitamin A	Vitamin C	Thiamine	Riboflavin	Niacin	Calcium	Iron
Appetizers														
Appetizing Antipasto (p. 8)	196	10	8	15	554	399	15	155	80	7	11	7	19	8
Artichokes with Citrus Butter (p. 58)	260	3	13	23	309	356	4	21	23	5	3	4	5	9
Cucumber-Spinach Dip with Crudités (p. 11)	15	0	1	1	30	30	1	2	1	0	1	0	2	0
Fried Asparagus (p. 107)	85	4	9	4	252	141	6	7	12	6	6	3	6	3
Fried Cucumber Chips (p. 101)	262	5	21	19	149	263	7	3	10	11	9	7	6	7
Sour-Cream-Dill Dip (p. 101)	66	1	2	6	20	50	2	5	1	1	3	0	4	0
Main Dishes														
Barbecue-Style Potatoes (p. 22)	660	23	92	23	1279	1236	35	14	63	17	20	36	29	75
Black Beans and Rice (p. 83)	379	24	64	3	763	789	37	0	11	58	13	23	11	31
Cantonese Beef with Hoisin Sauce (p. 91)	296	17	21	17	782	647	27	222	81	15	14	19	8	19
Carrot Soufflé (p. 114)	393	10	21	19	362	337	15	319	11	11	17	5	11	10
Cheesy Brussels Sprouts and Tofu (p. 68)	423	20	26	28	821	493	31	26	68	12	18	11	34	13
Cheesy Potato (p. 22)	489	17	79	13	270	1013	26	8	38	14	19	26	33	68
Chili-Cheese Potatoes (p. 22)	875	36	91	41	1340	1497	56	12	38	17	32	50	34	84
Crab- and Avocado-Stuffed Zucchini (p. 51)	282	13	10	23	355	829	20	41	22	16	9	17	6	10
Cream Cheese Potato (p. 22)	646	15	81	30	446	1016	23	16	43	17	16	29	11	67
Curried Chicken in Potatoes (p. 23)	540	25	85	12	681	1202	38	5	67	18	17	59	9	74
Curried Sausage-Stuffed Squash (p. 48)	499	17	63	22	859	1319	27	18	36	58	11	34	13	20
Curried Vegetables (p. 88)	347	12	44	14	332	555	18	246	115	20	7	25	10	19
Garden Potato (p. 22)	514	22	81	12	442	1088	33	9	43	14	22	27	30	69
German-Style Deep-Dish Pizza (p. 110)	499	24	42	27	1427	609	38	38	56	23	33	18	55	21
Greek Potato (p. 22)	411	12	85	4	231	1182	18	3	41	16	21	27	22	69
Herbed Bean Stew (p. 82)	358	15	48	13	925	855	23	15	37	39	20	18	19	28
Low-Cal Potato (p. 22)	387	11	84	1	92	1161	18	1	39	16	21	27	20	67

	Per Serving						Percent U.S. RDA Per Serving							
	Calories	Protein (g)	Carbohydrate (g)	Fat (g)	Sodium (mg)	Potassium (mg)	Protein	Vitamin A	Vitamin C	Thiamine	Riboflavin	Niacin	Calcium	Iron

Main Dishes (continued)

	Calories	Protein (g)	Carbohydrate (g)	Fat (g)	Sodium (mg)	Potassium (mg)	Protein	Vitamin A	Vitamin C	Thiamine	Riboflavin	Niacin	Calcium	Iron
Meat and Potatoes (p. 22)	559	33	85	10	158	1319	51	0	27	20	23	49	7	86
Pork and Pepper Stir-Fry (p. 91)	215	19	8	12	563	467	30	15	98	43	13	21	1	11
Potatoes with Shrimp Creole Topper (p. 20)	425	19	87	1	290	1373	29	14	48	18	13	30	13	76
Savory Stuffed Eggplant (p. 51)	317	26	27	12	782	834	40	122	48	21	20	22	33	20
Shrimp-Stuffed Artichokes (p. 16)	271	20	19	14	221	679	30	16	22	8	17	14	28	15
Try-a-Topper Taters (p. 22)	508	10	82	17	78	1089	15	13	39	15	18	26	15	67
Zucchini Soufflé (p. 115)	360	16	11	28	520	300	25	25	8	10	22	4	31	11

Salads

	Calories	Protein (g)	Carbohydrate (g)	Fat (g)	Sodium (mg)	Potassium (mg)	Protein	Vitamin A	Vitamin C	Thiamine	Riboflavin	Niacin	Calcium	Iron
Creamy Chayote (p. 17)	90	5	8	5	64	245	7	4	10	4	6	9	8	3
Creamy Curry-Vegetable Salad (p. 10)	125	4	10	9	33	298	7	3	16	4	5	2	6	8
Crunchy Jicama Salad (p. 10)	211	3	15	16	206	121	5	4	33	3	4	0	5	8
Tomato-Mushroom Salad (p. 11)	84	1	5	7	8	265	2	30	30	5	7	5	2	5
Wilted Spinach Salad (p. 56)	105	8	12	4	278	1057	12	222	57	13	26	12	19	28

Side Dishes

	Calories	Protein (g)	Carbohydrate (g)	Fat (g)	Sodium (mg)	Potassium (mg)	Protein	Vitamin A	Vitamin C	Thiamine	Riboflavin	Niacin	Calcium	Iron
Asparagus with Almond Sauce (p. 43)	89	3	5	7	79	278	5	14	24	6	8	5	4	4
Beer-Cheese Broccoli and Onion (p. 70)	146	7	9	10	273	304	10	25	65	5	11	3	16	4
Broccoli with Brie Sauce (p. 44)	101	5	6	7	178	274	8	25	73	4	11	3	8	4
Broiled Tomatoes (p. 33)	63	2	5	4	113	156	4	20	16	3	3	3	6	4
Calico Fritters (p. 106)	148	3	15	9	267	94	5	4	4	8	9	6	3	6
Cauliflower-Asparagus Stir-Fry (p. 86)	87	4	9	5	8	453	6	16	74	10	9	7	4	5
Cauliflower Supreme (p. 71)	167	5	10	13	277	299	7	24	57	6	8	3	11	5
Chayote-Rice Stir-Fry (p. 89)	172	6	25	6	306	347	9	8	39	12	9	11	8	10
Cheesy Beer-Batter Onion Rings (p. 104)	194	6	19	10	118	156	9	2	7	10	7	6	10	7
Cheesy Chokes and Leeks (p. 43)	128	5	19	4	91	425	8	5	12	12	8	6	15	17
Corn Relish (p. 58)	47	1	12	0	47	75	1	2	7	1	1	2	1	1
Creamed Parsnips and Peas (p. 44)	149	5	21	6	163	360	7	11	23	13	9	7	8	7
Creamy Caraway Cabbage (p. 70)	220	5	15	16	120	460	8	14	42	9	19	10	15	7
Creole-Style Vegetables (p. 57)	46	2	10	0	113	370	3	25	48	11	3	5	7	6
Crumb-Capped Green Beans (p. 16)	87	3	13	3	189	140	4	10	10	5	5	4	4	5
Curried Cauliflower Puree (p. 64)	18	2	4	0	11	269	2	0	63	4	2	2	2	3
Dilled Green Beans and Tomatoes (p. 89)	87	2	6	7	46	182	3	14	14	4	6	3	5	4
Eggplant Pizzas (p. 32)	133	8	10	7	376	180	12	10	6	6	7	5	20	5
French Fries (p. 107)	198	3	27	9	9	815	5	0	34	9	3	11	1	6
Fried Okra (p. 100)	229	5	14	17	85	199	8	9	11	10	7	5	6	7
German-Style Stuffed Turnips (p. 50)	134	4	13	8	425	294	6	7	29	5	6	3	11	4
Glazed Onions (p. 16)	126	2	17	6	64	259	3	5	39	6	1	1	4	5
Grilled Asparagus with Sorrel Dressing (p. 96)	135	5	6	11	94	406	7	26	45	9	10	7	6	5
Grilled Beets (p. 97)	266	2	41	12	222	481	3	9	23	4	2	3	3	10
Harvard Beets (p. 56)	86	2	15	3	169	357	2	2	13	3	1	2	2	6
Herbed Grilled Potatoes (p. 97)	221	3	26	12	126	777	5	9	32	8	3	11	1	6
Honeyed Rutabagas and Apples (p. 57)	144	1	23	6	109	358	2	5	29	6	2	3	5	3
Kohlrabi Bake (p. 94)	102	5	5	7	292	281	7	7	48	3	4	2	11	2
Lemon-Basil Carrots (p. 45)	99	1	11	6	97	359	2	612	13	7	4	5	3	3
Lemony Pepper Corn-on-the-Cob (p. 97)	159	3	18	10	102	264	5	12	8	12	3	8	1	4

	Per Serving					Percent U.S. RDA Per Serving								
	Calories	Protein (g)	Carbohydrate (g)	Fat (g)	Sodium (mg)	Potassium (mg)	Protein	Vitamin A	Vitamin C	Thiamine	Riboflavin	Niacin	Calcium	Iron
Side Dishes *(continued)*														
Mashed Potatoes (p. 65)	141	3	21	6	106	624	4	4	37	7	3	8	1	5
Mexican Potatoes (p. 64)	136	3	23	4	160	667	5	7	52	8	5	9	5	5
New England Baked Beans (p. 82)	226	9	37	5	141	636	14	0	2	18	6	6	10	22
New Potatoes with Mustard Sauce (p. 45)	193	5	25	8	340	728	7	6	27	9	8	9	9	6
Orange Carrots and Sprouts (p. 17)	116	4	16	5	68	518	6	320	86	11	6	6	5	9
Oriental Beans (p. 96)	36	2	8	0	519	181	3	8	12	3	4	4	2	6
Oriental Turnips (p. 65)	91	1	9	6	222	245	2	4	28	3	2	3	4	3
Oriental Vegetable Tempura (p. 106)	160	5	19	8	90	330	8	10	45	10	15	10	2	10
Orzo- and Feta-Stuffed Pepper Shells (p. 50)	212	7	21	12	410	333	11	22	129	15	12	9	13	11
Pea Pods and Summer Squash (p. 57)	79	2	7	6	95	172	3	8	27	6	4	3	4	4
Potato Chips (p. 107)	198	3	27	9	9	815	5	0	34	9	3	11	1	6
Sesame Broccoli (p. 14)	97	4	7	7	91	396	6	42	130	6	9	4	6	7
Shoestring Potatoes (p. 107)	198	3	27	9	9	815	5	0	34	9	3	11	1	6
Southern Sweet Potatoes (p. 62)	298	4	48	11	215	395	5	687	48	12	15	6	4	7
South-of-the-Border Taters (p. 23)	422	9	85	6	474	1085	14	9	63	15	12	27	7	68
Spaghetti Squash with Tomato-Dill Sauce (p. 54)	86	2	13	3	288	444	3	22	27	70	61	3	2	6
Sweet 'n' Sour Vegetables (p. 88)	86	2	13	4	15	323	3	2	48	6	11	9	4	6
Sweet-Sour Cabbage (p. 40)	134	3	31	1	258	600	5	51	186	8	5	5	10	12
Swiss Cheese and Bacon Potatoes (p. 71)	261	11	24	14	232	706	17	7	27	12	13	11	22	6
Volcano Potatoes (p. 65)	193	4	21	11	209	640	7	8	26	7	5	8	6	5
Whipped Rutabagas (p. 64)	159	3	11	12	234	443	4	11	35	7	6	4	10	4
Soups														
Autumnfest Soup (p. 76)	189	5	16	13	471	619	8	17	17	13	8	13	11	7
Broccoli-Cheese Soup (p. 77)	335	15	12	26	455	467	23	40	78	7	21	11	40	6
Celery-Spinach Soup (p. 28)	79	6	5	3	505	394	9	39	13	3	7	9	14	7
Cheesy Mushroom Soup (p. 76)	327	6	8	31	394	293	9	24	3	5	19	13	9	6
Chilled Spinach Soup (p. 74)	168	8	11	10	428	603	12	81	20	6	19	10	21	10
Corkscrew Vegetable Soup (p. 28)	81	4	13	1	465	266	6	115	5	9	8	13	3	5
Creamy Pea Soup (p. 76)	171	8	14	10	427	323	12	20	19	15	10	14	7	8
French Onion Soup (p. 26)	402	17	34	22	1168	452	26	14	18	17	15	15	39	12
Hearty Potato Soup (p. 77)	333	11	30	19	717	687	16	91	18	20	14	19	11	6
Jambalaya Soup (p. 29)	128	15	13	2	506	597	24	20	42	23	7	18	11	14
Minestrone (p. 83)	284	16	43	6	576	703	25	109	10	30	16	18	20	24
Oriental Chicken-Vegetable Soup (p. 28)	114	16	6	3	950	532	24	120	12	6	13	38	7	12
Quick Succotash-Squash Soup (p. 29)	199	10	40	2	544	894	16	13	28	18	8	21	6	13
Succotash-Squash Soup (p. 29)	173	9	34	2	502	781	14	9	22	16	7	19	6	12
Vegetarian Chili (p. 80)	411	22	37	20	1176	1203	35	50	113	29	21	39	33	27
Miscellaneous														
Cream Cheese Frosting (p. 36)	164	1	22	8	80	14	1	7	0	0	1	0	1	1
Mustard Sauce (p. 101)	46	1	2	4	129	61	2	3	0	1	3	0	5	0
Sunshine Carrot Cake (p. 36)	328	4	47	14	145	129	7	144	4	11	8	6	6	8
Sweet and Sour Sauce (p. 106)	60	0	15	0	170	75	0	0	0	0	0	0	0	2
Whole Wheat-Zucchini Bread (p. 37)	201	3	30	8	104	108	5	2	3	8	4	4	2	6

A-B

Appetizers
  Appetizing Antipasto, 8
  Artichokes with Citrus
    Butter, 58
  Calico Fritters, 106
  Celery-Spinach Soup, 28
  Cheesy Mushroom Soup, 76
  Chilled Spinach Soup, 74
  Corn Relish, 58
  Cucumber-Spinach Dip with
    Crudités, 11
  Fried Asparagus, 107
  Fried Cucumber Chips, 101
  Sour-Cream-Dill Dip, 101
Artichokes, Shrimp-Stuffed, 16
Artichokes with Citrus Butter, 58
Asparagus
  Asparagus with Almond
    Sauce, 43
  Cauliflower-Asparagus
    Stir-Fry, 86
  Dilled Green Beans and
    Tomatoes, 89
  Fried Asparagus, 107
  Grilled Asparagus with Sorrel
    Dressing, 96
Autumnfest Soup, 76
Barbecues
  Grilled Asparagus with Sorrel
    Dressing, 96
  Grilled Beets, 97
  Herbed Grilled Potatoes, 97
  Kohlrabi Bake, 94
  Lemony Pepper Corn-on-the-
    Cob, 97
  Oriental Beans, 96
  Testing coals for
    temperature, 95
Barbecue-Style Potatoes, 22
Beans (See also Dry Beans)
  Crumb-Capped Green
    Beans, 16
  Dilled Green Beans and
    Tomatoes, 89
  Oriental Beans, 96

Beans *(continued)*
  Oriental Vegetable
    Tempura, 106
  Quick Succotash-Squash
    Soup, 29
  Succotash-Squash Soup, 29
Beer-Cheese Broccoli and
  Onion, 70
Beets, Grilled, 97
Beets, Harvard, 56
Black Beans and Rice, 83
Bread, Whole Wheat-Zucchini, 37
Broccoli
  Appetizing Antipasto, 8
  Beer-Cheese Broccoli and
    Onion, 70
  Broccoli-Cheese Soup, 77
  Broccoli with Brie Sauce, 44
  Cantonese Beef with Hoisin
    Sauce, 91
  Oriental Vegetable
    Tempura, 106
  Sesame Broccoli, 14
Broiled Tomatoes, 33
Brussels Sprouts
  Cheesy Brussels Sprouts and
    Tofu, 68
  Curried Vegetables, 88
  Orange Carrots and
    Sprouts, 17

C

Cabbage
  Creamy Caraway Cabbage, 70
  Sweet 'n' Sour Vegetables, 88
  Sweet-Sour Cabbage, 40
Cake, Sunshine Carrot, 36
Calico Fritters, 106
Cantonese Beef with Hoisin
  Sauce, 91
Carrots
  Appetizing Antipasto, 8
  Cantonese Beef with Hoisin
    Sauce, 91
  Carrot Soufflé, 114

Carrots *(continued)*
  Curried Vegetables, 88
  Lemon-Basil Carrots, 45
  Orange Carrots and
    Sprouts, 17
  Sunshine Carrot Cake, 36
Cauliflower
  Appetizing Antipasto, 8
  Broccoli with Brie Sauce, 44
  Cauliflower-Asparagus
    Stir-Fry, 86
  Cauliflower Supreme, 71
  Curried Cauliflower Puree, 64
Celery-Spinach Soup, 28
Chayote, Creamy, 17
Chayote-Rice Stir-Fry, 89
Cheeses
  Beer-Cheese Broccoli and
    Onion, 70
  Broccoli-Cheese Soup, 77
  Broccoli with Brie Sauce, 44
  Cauliflower Supreme, 71
  Cheesy Beer-Batter Onion
    Rings, 104
  Cheesy Brussels Sprouts and
    Tofu, 68
  Cheesy Chokes and Leeks, 43
  Cheesy Mushroom Soup, 76
  Cheesy Potato, 22
  Cream Cheese Potato, 22
  French Onion Soup, 26
  Garden Potato, 22
  German-Style Deep-Dish
    Pizza, 110
  Orzo- and Feta-Stuffed Pepper
    Shells, 50
  Swiss Cheese and Bacon
    Potatoes, 71
Chicken
  Curried Chicken in
    Potatoes, 23
  Meat and Potatoes, 22
  Oriental Chicken-Vegetable
    Soup, 28
Chili-Cheese Potatoes, 22
Chilled Spinach Soup, 74
Corkscrew Vegetable Soup, 28

Corn
  Corn Relish, 58
  Lemony Pepper Corn-on-the-
    Cob, 97
  Quick Succotash-Squash
    Soup, 29
  Succotash-Squash Soup, 29
Crab- and Avocado-Stuffed
  Zucchini, 51
Cream Cheese Frosting, 36
Cream Cheese Potato, 22
Creamed Parsnips and Peas, 44
Creamy Caraway Cabbage, 70
Creamy Chayote, 17
Creamy Curry-Vegetable
  Salad, 10
Creamy Pea Soup, 76
Creole-Style Vegetables, 57
Crumb-Capped Green Beans, 16
Crunchy Jicama Salad, 10
Cucumber Chips, Fried, 101
Cucumber-Spinach Dip with
  Crudités, 11
Curry
  Creamy Curry-Vegetable
    Salad, 10
  Curried Cauliflower Puree, 64
  Curried Chicken in
    Potatoes, 23
  Curried Sausage-Stuffed
    Squash, 48
  Curried Vegetables, 88

D-E

Daikon
  Creamy Curry-Vegetable
    Salad, 10
  Oriental Chicken-Vegetable
    Soup, 28
Dilled Green Beans and
  Tomatoes, 89

Doneness Tests
  Crisp-tender, 15
  Dry beans, 81
  Soufflés, 114
Draining off fat, 48
Dry Beans
  Black Beans and Rice, 83
  Herbed Bean Stew, 82
  Minestrone, 83
  New England Baked Beans, 82
  Testing for doneness, 81
  Vegetarian Chili, 80
Eggplant, Savory Stuffed, 51
Eggplant Pizzas, 32
Eggs
  Carrot Soufflé, 114
  Separating eggs, 114
  Stiffly beating egg whites, 114
  Zucchini Soufflé, 115

F-L

French Fries, 107
French Onion Soup, 26
Fried Asparagus, 107
Fried Cucumber Chips, 101
Fried Okra, 100
Fritters, Calico, 106
Garden Potato, 22
German-Style Deep-Dish
  Pizza, 110
German-Style Stuffed Turnips, 50
Glazed Onions, 16
Greek Potato, 22
Grilled Asparagus with Sorrel
  Dressing, 96
Grilled Beets, 97
Harvard Beets, 56
Hearty Potato Soup, 77
Herbed Bean Stew, 82
Herbed Grilled Potatoes, 97
Honeyed Rutabagas and
  Apples, 57
Jambalaya Soup, 29
Jerusalem Artichokes
  Cheesy Chokes and Leeks, 43

Jicama Salad, Crunchy, 10
Julienne vegetables, 9
Kohlrabi Bake, 94
Leeks, Cheesy Chokes and, 43
Lemon-Basil Carrots, 45
Lemony Pepper Corn-on-the-
  Cob, 97
Low-Cal Potato, 22

M

Main Dishes (See also Chicken,
    Pork)
  Barbecue-Style Potatoes, 22
  Broccoli-Cheese Soup, 77
  Cantonese Beef with Hoisin
    Sauce, 91
  Carrot Soufflé, 114
  Cheesy Brussels Sprouts and
    Tofu, 68
  Cheesy Potato, 22
  Chili-Cheese Potatoes, 22
  Crab- and Avocado-Stuffed
    Zucchini, 51
  Cream Cheese Potato, 22
  Curried Vegetables, 88
  French Onion Soup, 26
  Garden Potato, 22
  Greek Potato, 22
  Hearty Potato Soup, 77
  Herbed Bean Stew, 82
  Jambalaya Soup, 29
  Low-Cal Potato, 22
  Meat and Potatoes, 22
  Minestrone, 83
  Potatoes with Shrimp Creole
    Topper, 20
  Savory Stuffed Eggplant, 51
  Shrimp-Stuffed Artichokes, 16
  Try-a-Topper Taters, 22
  Vegetarian Chili, 80
  Zucchini Soufflé, 115

Mashed Potatoes, 65
Meat and Potatoes, 22
Mexican Potatoes, 64
Microwave
  Artichokes with Citrus
    Butter, 58
  Cheesy Brussels Sprouts and
    Tofu, 68
  Corn Relish, 58
  Creole-Style Vegetables, 57
  Harvard Beets, 56
  Honeyed Rutabagas and
    Apples, 57
  Pea Pods and Summer
    Squash, 57
  Spaghetti Squash with
    Tomato-Dill Sauce, 54
  Wilted Spinach Salad, 56
Minestrone, 83
Mushrooms
  Calico Fritters, 106
  Chayote-Rice Stir-Fry, 89
  Cheesy Mushroom Soup, 76
  Corkscrew Vegetable Soup, 28
  Creamy Caraway Cabbage, 70
  Oriental Chicken-Vegetable
    Soup, 28
  Oriental Vegetable
    Tempura, 106
  Sweet 'n' Sour Vegetables, 88
  Tomato-Mushroom Salad, 11
  Wilted Spinach Salad, 56
Mustard Sauce, 101

N-O

New England Baked Beans, 82
New Potatoes with Mustard
  Sauce, 45
Okra
  Creole-Style Vegetables, 57
  Fried Okra, 100
  Jambalaya Soup, 29

Onions
  Beer-Cheese Broccoli and
    Onion, 70
  Cheesy-Beer Batter Onion
    Rings, 104
  French Onion Soup, 26
  Glazed Onions, 16
Orange Carrots and Sprouts, 17
Oriental Beans, 96
Oriental Chicken-Vegetable
  Soup, 28
Oriental Turnips, 65
Oriental Vegetable Tempura, 106
Orzo- and Feta-Stuffed Pepper
  Shells, 50

P-R

Pan-frying vegetables, 100
Parsnips
  Creamed Parsnips and
    Peas, 44
  Creamy Curry-Vegetable
    Salad, 10
Pea Pods
  Cantonese Beef with Hoisin
    Sauce, 91
  Pea Pods and Summer
    Squash, 57
  Sweet 'n' Sour Vegetables, 88
Peas, Creamed Parsnips and, 44
Pea Soup, Creamy, 76
Peppers
  Curried Vegetables, 88
  Orzo- and Feta-Stuffed Pepper
    Shells, 50
  Pork and Pepper Stir-Fry, 91
Pizza, German-Style Deep-
  Dish, 110
Pizzas, Eggplant, 32

Pork
  Black Beans and Rice, 83
  Curried Sausage-Stuffed
    Squash, 48
  Hearty Potato Soup, 77
  Jambalaya Soup, 29
  Pork and Pepper Stir-Fry, 91
Potatoes
  Barbecue-Style Potatoes, 22
  Cheesy Potato, 22
  Chili-Cheese Potatoes, 22
  Cream Cheese Potato, 22
  Curried Chicken in
    Potatoes, 23
  French Fries, 107
  Garden Potato, 22
  Greek Potato, 22
  Hearty Potato Soup, 77
  Herbed Grilled Potatoes, 97
  Low-Cal Potato, 22
  Mashed Potatoes, 65
  Meat and Potatoes, 22
  Mexican Potatoes, 64
  Micro-Baked Potatoes, 21
  New Potatoes with Mustard
    Sauce, 45
  Potato Chips, 107
  Potatoes with Shrimp Creole
    Topper, 20
  Shoestring Potatoes, 107
  Southern Sweet Potatoes, 62
  South-of-the-Border Taters, 23
  Swiss Cheese and Bacon
    Potatoes, 71
  Try-a-Topper Taters, 22
  Volcano Potatoes, 65
Pureeing vegetables, 74
Quick Succotash-Squash
  Soup, 29
Rutabagas
  Herbed Bean Stew, 82
  Honeyed Rutabagas and
    Apples, 57
  Whipped Rutabagas, 64

S

Salads
Creamy Chayote, 17
Creamy Curry-Vegetable
Salad, 10
Crunchy Jicama Salad, 10
Tomato-Mushroom Salad, 11
Wilted Spinach Salad, 56
Sauerkraut
German-Style Deep-Dish
Pizza, 110
German-Style Stuffed
Turnips, 50
Savory Stuffed Eggplant, 51
Sesame Broccoli, 14
Shoestring Potatoes, 107
Shrimp Creole Topper, Potatoes
with, 20
Shrimp-Stuffed Artichokes, 16
Soufflé, Carrot, 114
Soufflé, Zucchini, 115
Soups
Autumnfest Soup, 76
Broccoli-Cheese Soup, 77
Celery-Spinach Soup, 28
Cheesy Mushroom Soup, 76
Chilled Spinach Soup, 74
Corkscrew Vegetable Soup, 28
Creamy Pea Soup, 76
French Onion Soup, 26
Hearty Potato Soup, 77
Jambalaya Soup, 29
Minestrone, 83
Oriental Chicken-Vegetable
Soup, 28
Quick Succotash-Squash
Soup, 29
Succotash-Squash Soup, 29
Vegetarian Chili, 80
Sour-Cream-Dill Dip, 101
Southern Sweet Potatoes, 62
South-of-the-Border Taters, 23
Spaghetti Squash with Tomato-
Dill Sauce, 54

Spinach
Celery-Spinach Soup, 28
Chilled Spinach Soup, 74
Creamy Pea Soup, 76
Cucumber-Spinach Dip with
Crudités, 11
Wilted Spinach Salad, 56
Squash (See also Zucchini)
Appetizing Antipasto, 8
Autumnfest Soup, 76
Curried Sausage-Stuffed
Squash, 48
Pea Pods and Summer
Squash, 57
Spaghetti Squash with
Tomato-Dill Sauce, 54
Succotash-Squash Soup, 29
Sunshine Carrot Cake, 36
Sweet and Sour Sauce, 106
Sweet 'n' Sour Vegetables, 88
Sweet Potatoes, Southern, 62
Swiss Cheese and Bacon
Potatoes, 71

T-Z

Tofu
Cheesy Brussels Sprouts and
Tofu, 68
Curried Vegetables, 88
Oriental Chicken-Vegetable
Soup, 28
Tomatoes
Appetizing Antipasto, 8
Broiled Tomatoes, 33
Creole-Style Vegetables, 57
Dilled Green Beans and
Tomatoes, 89
German-Style Deep-Dish
Pizza, 110
Pork and Pepper Stir-Fry, 91
Spaghetti Squash with
Tomato-Dill Sauce, 54
Tomato-Mushroom Salad, 11
Try-a-Topper Taters, 22

Turnips, German-Style
Stuffed, 50
Turnips, Oriental, 65
Vegetarian Chili, 80
Venting plastic wrap in
microwave cooking, 54
Volcano Potatoes, 65
Whipped Rutabagas, 64
Whole Wheat-Zucchini Bread, 37
Wilted Spinach Salad, 56
Zucchini
Appetizing Antipasto, 8
Chayote-Rice Stir-Fry, 89
Crab- and Avocado-Stuffed
Zucchini, 51
Creamy Curry-Vegetable
Salad, 10
Oriental Vegetable
Tempura, 106
Whole Wheat-Zucchini
Bread, 37
Zucchini Soufflé, 115

Tips

Attention Microwave Owners!, 23
Cutting Edge, The, 10
Inside Scoop on Artichokes,
The, 17
Micro-Baked Potatoes, 21
Overnight Soaking, 82
Stir-Frying without a Wok, 89